Five Minutes to Happiness

Maxwell Maltz, MD

MEDIA

Published 2018 by Gildan Media LLC
aka G&D Media
www.GandDmedia.com

Copyright © 1967, 2016, 2018
Five Minutes to Happiness By Maxwell Maltz, M.D.

ISBN: 978-1-7225-0031-3

CONTENTS

FOREWORD

When I ask people I coach in the principles of *Psycho-Cybernetics* to give a success experiences they're proud of, it's no longer surprising when the only answer I hear is . . . silence. Alternatively, if I flip the question and ask for a recollection of "happy moments," oftentimes I immediately witness a cavalcade of answers filled with joy and enthusiasm.

All human beings can instantaneously recall successes when they understand that a happy moment equals a success experience. The first time you tied your shoes, learned to write your name, were able to utter the colloquial expressions for your mother and father, speak a language (including the one you learned first), independently fed and clothed yourself for the first time, as well as crawled, rolled over, walked, ran and rode a bicycle – all of these are happy moments that you didn't take for granted at the time.

You may think these happy moments are inconsequential now, but they're not. How do I know? I know because when you answer the following question: Would you rather NOT be able to walk, talk, tie your shoes and write your name? – you will vociferously argue in favor of the activities you've been blasé about.

Yes, the activities mentioned above are also success experiences. Let's simply view them as happy moments for now, which is the subject of this sensational book, *Five Minutes to Happiness*, written by our mentor, Dr. Maxwell Maltz.

Undoubtedly, the moment I was first introduced to Dr. Maltz teachings on *Psycho-Cybernetics*, my life did an about-face. I learned to use my memory and my imagination simultaneously. I discovered that picturing the successful achievement of a goal was usually not enough to create the desired outcome.

Dr. Maltz stressed that it is not just the power of your imagination that is vitally important; it's also your memories of positive moments wherein you were in a state of flow. Your memories are the fuel in your brain-tank. If you refuse to acknowledge the existence of these memories, you're running on empty before you begin. But when you fill your consciousness with a plethora of positivity regarding the past, regardless of how long ago it took place, you are magnetizing more of what you truly want into your life.

I wholeheartedly believe *Five Minutes to Happiness* will cause an awakening within you, filling you with the desire to rekindle the passion contained in your positive memories and using it to catapult you toward the creation of many more.

For even more assistance in your journey of self-discovery, visit the ***Psycho-Cybernetics.com*** website for our bonus email tips as well as for inquiries about coaching, seminars and other opportunities.

—Matt Furey
President of *The Psycho-Cybernetics Foundation*
Psycho-Cybernetics.com

CHAPTER 1

THE TOOLS AND EQUIPMENT FOR HAPPINESS

PART OF AN EXTERNAL EXPRESSION of happiness is a smile on the face. It is the reverse of a frown. A frown is a symbol of tension, a smile an expression of relaxation.

It is obvious then that the essential ingredient of happiness is an atmosphere conducive to relaxation. Relaxation like tension is a state of mind, which means that we can form a habit of relaxation. We do this with the imagination. The whole art of living is the outcome of the use or abuse of the imagination. To use the imagination constructively we build a room where we can do nothing but relax.

As Americans we are wont to indulge in all sorts of pastimes, and one that tickles our fancy very much is the art of building a room—ah by ourselves. Wherever or whenever we can, we do it ourselves. We build the walls, the doors; we put in the window, the closet, the shelves. We paint the walls and the ceiling and we carpet the floor. Some of us even build the furniture and various other conveniences that go with it. The business of doing it ourselves runs into hundreds of millions of dollars annually, proving that this national pastime is here to stay, simply because there is pleasure in it.

Building a room by ourselves, and assembling all the paraphernalia that go with it, merely symbolizes an extension of the physical and spiritual freedom that we have earned by struggle and love so dearly that we are prepared to die to protect it. So we have every right to pamper ourselves, expressing our love of freedom particularly when it comes to our home. We know that it is easier to pull down than to build, but building is a constructive challenge we gladly accept, for beyond the material reward is the pleasure that goes with any creative process. And when this room is done, we know that it is all ours and that we are king in it.

MY NEPHEW'S ROOM

The other day I went to Long Island to have dinner with my nephew and his wife. They guided me to a comfortable chair and pretty Lila handed me a drink.

"Where are the kids?" I asked.

"They're upstairs. They've had their dinner."

Both boys, eight and seven, and the twins, girls, two years of age, heard my voice and down they came. They rushed over to me urging me to repeat a lesson in How to Whistle, complaining that they were not as yet masters of the art. I put the index and ring fingers of my right hand in my mouth and blew a tremendous whistle. They jumped with joy, then tried to do it themselves but failed. Suddenly they climbed all over me, mussed my hair, and put their fingers in my mouth to get a more accurate idea how it was done. Their dog, a powerful boxer, suddenly made his appearance and, thinking that the children were being molested, barked and jumped on me in an effort to get me away from them.

My nephew Harold rushed the children and their canine buddy up the steps, and I closed my eyes and suppressed a sigh. Suddenly I heard a shot. It was a gun all right, I said to myself, then tried to doze off. A minute later I heard the shot again. Now I listened for it and sure enough I heard it again and again and again.

"What's going on, Harold?"

"Nothing, Unc. Your nephew Mae is downstairs in the basement."

"What is he doing there? What's all the noise?"

"He's building! He's making a playroom out of the basement."

"But what's all the shooting?" I asked.

"Come down and see."

I went down and saw Mac holding a plank of wood against the wall with his left hand and pointing the gun in his right band against the wood; then he pulled the trigger. He examined the nail he had just fired through the wood into the wall, smiled contentedly, wiped the sweat off his face, greeted me peremptorily, then proceeded to saw the last plank of wood that would finish the job. And it was as beautiful a job indeed as if done by a professional. I knew it would be a wonderful playroom for the children and for the adults as well.

A SPECIAL ROOM FOR ALL OF US

But I also know of building a room in a much easier way despite the fact it was easy for Mac to do it. The room I have in mind does not need any wood planks or guns; nor does it require labor and sweat. It is there for the asking and we can all have it. We build this room with our imagination . . . nothing else.

When we are finished with the excessive tensions of the day—and they will always be there, in the very nature of things—we can replenish our youthful vigor by simply walking through a door—any door of our home into this room . . . this new room, which is the room next door. Of course, it is an imaginary room, a room in our mind. Open the door and walk into it. And a beautiful room it is—all built for us—a solarium, with the sun streaming through it, a veritable garden, filled with flowers and with a fountain bubbling in the middle.

There's a chair waiting for us. We sit down and relax for a while. We look at the flashing waters of the fountain, breathe in the perfume of the flowers. We rest for a while every day—for just five minutes . . . five minutes that will bring happiness.

To summarize:

1. Imagination is essential equipment for happiness.

2. So is relaxation—one of our greatest assets.

3. A smile on the face is an expression of relaxation, the reverse of a frown, which is a symbol of tension. It is well to remember what Dale Carnegie said: "You don't feel like smiling? Then what? First, force yourself to smile. If you are alone, force yourself, to whistle or hum a tune or sing. Act as if you were already happy, and that will tend to make you happy."

4. To use the imagination constructively we build a room in our mind where we do one thing and one thing only . . . Relax!

CHAPTER 2

HOW TO RELAX

NOW THAT WE ARE SITTING in this room of our mind, we look out the window and see many sights. Scenes of the past and scenes of the present. We see a day of yesterday, a day in a small town. The phone rings once or twice. The country doctor wakes up slowly, weary from overwork. He gets to the phone, listens, then says he is on his way. Soon he gets into his buggy with his instrument bag, says "Giddap" to his old dependable horse, and we see him moving over the hills in the rain toward some distant village miles away where a pregnant woman, writhing in pain, is anxiously waiting for him to help bring her child into the world.

Now we see a day of the present, fast automobiles moving back and forth on the highways. We see the rush and the hurry. We see people enter a jet. One of them is a doctor anxious to get to a sick patient hundreds of miles away. And perhaps I'm on the plane too, flying down to Latin America to take care of someone injured somewhere.

TENSION

Naturally the jet age has its many advantages, but on the other hand the rapid pace at which we live seems to have accelerated our tensions, our social, emotional, and economic conflicts. We seem to get them much faster. That being the case, there is no reason why we cannot learn how to relax, and we don't have to do it on the double.

How do we relax? Well, in the first place the reverse of relaxation is tension and this tension can be expressed both externally and internally. Externally it is expressed in our face, our voice, our chest, and our hands and even our feet. Internally it may be expressed in a spasm of our stomach or our intestines, or even in our blood vessels.

Watch our face under tension. It shows that the muscles are tense; they are contracting without purpose, or more than they should for the problem confronting us. Our forehead is corrugated into a frown and our upper lip is raised; we are on the first lap of developing a crying spell, but we repress it. Continual tension unreleased may cause the muscles around our eyes to twitch. It may make us breathe heavily with our chest muscles, when under normal intelligent conditions we should be breathing from our abdomen, that is, with our diaphragm, slow and easy. If our mouth is not open, we are gritting our teeth or biting our lips, and we are overworking those muscles around our chin. Our voice is not our own because we are uncertain, worried, and timid. Since we are not sure of ourselves, our voice is not sure of itself; it comes out differently, weak and unsteady and unnatural. We fidget with our hands, we roll our fingers, we clench our fist, punch our palm, crack our knuckles or tap our fingers on the table. We talk fast as if we are running and when we sit down we are tapping our foot against the floor or shaking our knee.

THE CURE

Being aware of this unnecessary abuse of our energy and musculature is not necessarily the cure. Some people who try to overcome insomnia by counting sheep in bed at night often spend a sleepless night making sure they are exhausted.

One of the ways to release our tensions and feel relaxed and calm is to realize that our external muscles are working overtime only because our mind is disturbed with problems which we are afraid defy solution that can help us. We must go to the source of the trouble, to our mind. And it may be of value to us if we imagine our mind as having a face, a body, a voice, and hands and feet all its own.

If we can picture this, then we will see a frown of confusion and worry on the face of our mind. We will see teeth gritted and jaw firm. Now we open our mouth, I mean the mouth of our mind and we smile ever so gently. We will relax then because we cannot have a tense face with an open mouth and with a slight smile on it. We release the tension in the hands of our mind by opening up those clenched fists, so that we can spread our fingers and see the palms of our hands. It will take the pressure off those tired muscles and give us the feeling that we can be the master of the situation after all.

We must never let the feet of our mind run away with us; we hold them in check. They are not the feet of Olympic runners; they don't have to win a race. See them walking straight and secure, and with dignity. Dignity belongs to us; we are entitled to it. We don't abuse it by having it carry unnecessarily a carload of tensions that can break its back. Now see, that when we walk with dignity we let our mind breathe with dignity too, not as if the oxygen has been taken away from us. And now, listen to our mind speak. Let it be our voice, our voice when we are calm, collected, and know what we are doing. And this is what we will hear our voice say:

"Look, friend, tensions are made for us to overcome. We are not living in a vacuum. So we must do that extra job for ourselves. And the best time to do this extra job is during those eight hours when we are away from work, those eight hours of rest before we go to bed. We use five minutes—only five minutes in the room of our mind as we are doing now—when we take stock of ourselves. We think of our assets too, not merely of our shortcomings. We think of ways of improving ourselves and the best way we can do that is by trying to improve the situations of others who may be involved in our tensions with us. Tensions are pliable if we do not let them overpower us. We can bend them to our will a bit if our will is honest and does not hurt others. We must be proud of ourselves instead of ashamed of ourselves; proud that we are human beings born to overcome obstacles rather than to perish under them. We must realize once and for all that we are here in this world to succeed, not fail.

"And finally as we sit in the room of our mind, and look through the window, we see a geyser outside. And this geyser is blowing off steam. We let this be a symbol for us as we sit in this room for only five minutes, for releasing the tensions within us to break the electric circuit of distress for only five minutes . . . to let the tensions evaporate from us like the steam from the geyser."

It is well then to remember that we begin to walk on the road to happiness when we learn the art of relaxation, when we learn that relaxation is a habit we all can acquire, a healthy habit every day like brushing our teeth.

1. We utilize only five minutes of our daily eight-hour period of rest to sit in the room of our mind where we take stock of our assets as well as of our liabilities.
2. One of our great liabilities is that we inhibit ourselves from accomplishing our daily goal when we are fearful of failure.
3. We remember our past successes, to give us confidence.
4. We all live under pressure and the business of living effectively is to stand up to the tensions of the day. We do not let them overpower us.
5. We must learn to be proud of ourselves instead of ashamed of ourselves.
6. We get into the habit of opening our mouths a bit and we smile ever so slightly. We cannot be tense then.
7. We open our clenched fists to see the palms of our hands.
8. We must not run away with ourselves. We remember to walk with dignity. Dignity is one of our greatest assets. Self-respect is the power within us that makes us stand up to tension, to strengthen our emotional muscles.

9. Our self-respect guides us toward relaxation . . . instills in us the desire to improve ourselves . . . gives quality to our voice. It teaches us to be calm, collected, know what we are doing, which is the way to begin the habit of relaxation.

10. We see a geyser outside the room of our mind—a geyser letting off steam, a symbol for us of breaking the electric circuit of distress for only five minutes and renewing our belief in ourselves.

11. We are here in this world to succeed not to fail. As Disraeli put it: "The secret of success is constancy to purpose."

CHAPTER 3

THE STRANGER WITHIN

WE MEET STRANGERS every day of our lives wherever we go, but did it ever occur to us that we do not go alone, that there is a stranger, a particular stranger, that keeps us company all the time?

You are now seated in the room of your mind and you look out of the window. I am the person you see walking. I am walking alone. Or am I? A stranger is walking with me even though you don't see him. This stranger is the closest to me, closer than a wife, a child, a parent, or a friend. He is the stranger within me . . . the stranger within all of us, and the reason be is a stranger is that we don't know him, that we are unaware of his presence, unaware what his function is.

It is important to get to know him better because if we do, be can become our best friend, guide us and make us happy. We must be sincere with this stranger. If we ignore this stranger or don't understand him, he may become our worst enemy.

Who is this stranger within me, within all of us, a stranger who is the key to happiness? Let me tell you. Do you know that we have a self-image behind our face? This inner self-image has a face and a body of its own even if we don't see it. It is the face and the body of our mind, which dominates our life. It is our inner Siamese twin from whom we cannot escape . . . a twin who controls our life, our destiny, because whether we realize it or not we do what he tells us. This self-image is the heartbeat of our mind, the built-in clock that ticks away the hours of happiness or sorrow, depending on our understanding of him. He is our sentimental thermostat that regulates our behavior toward others and toward ourselves.

WE ARE OUR OWN PLASTIC SURGEON

How do we get to know and understand our self-image? Well, in the first place, we must realize that whether we are conscious of it or not, we have an image of ourselves, or concept of the sort of person we think we are. This has been built up from the beliefs about ourselves and these beliefs are there as a result of our past experiences, our successes and failures, our joys and sorrows, and the way other people react to us. Thus in a way, we are our own plastic surgeons and inwardly construct a picture of ourselves. Once a belief goes into this picture, true or false, we accept it as true and proceed to behave as if it were true.

This does two things:
1. We act, behave, and feel according to what we consider this self-image to be and we do not deviate from this pattern. We act according to what we conceive we are and in no other way. If we conceive ourselves as a "success type" person from a concept derived from our past successes, we will find ways of succeeding in our present undertaking. Without realizing it we will invoke the memory of past successes, will remember our self-confidence, self-respect, self-acceptance then, and use these positive qualities in our present undertaking.

On the other hand, if we consider ourselves a "failure type" person because of our past failures which inhibit us with fear in our present undertaking, we will without realizing it find some way to fail, despite everything, in order to be consistent with the picture we have of our self image. The stranger within us is the base upon which we build our behavior personality and we respond to life according to the dictates of our self image.

A girl who thinks she is unattractive will do things to prove she is unattractive. She invites rejection in order to satisfy the stranger within her, in order to satisfy her own evaluation of herself. Tell her that it is only an idea in her mind and that with the proper care of her face, her hair, her clothing, she can be attractive, she will not believe you until you can prove to her that she can change her self-image.

2. The stranger within us can be changed no matter what our image may be and through this constructive change we can start a new life which puts us on the road to happiness. It is impossible to think positively about any undertaking as long as we have a negative image of ourselves. But if the stranger within us is changed by us into a friend, into a satisfactory image, we achieve the ends or goal consistent with this self-image.

A GREAT DISCOVERY

I came to this realization in my practice as a plastic surgeon. Removing a scar or deformity of the face changed personality. A boy with protruding ears who was ridiculed by playmates avoided them to avoid humiliation. He retired within himself. When his ears were corrected the cause for his embarrassment was removed and he played again with his classmates and assumed a normal role in life.

A salesman whose face was scarred in an auto accident suddenly had a distorted image of himself. He lost confidence in himself. He became bitter and hostile, directing his energies to himself instead of to the outside world. Bringing his face back to normal brought his self-image back to normal.

But I found in a small percentage of cases that a disfigurement removed didn't change personality. One of these, patients, a woman whose nose was broken, did not see any change when the nose was repaired. I showed her the pictures taken before the surgery. She admitted she looked better but felt as she bad before the operation. She had an inner deformity, an inner scar. She had a distorted self image—a distorted stranger within—that she had unknowingly put there as a result of her past failures in life. Making her see that, eventually changed the stranger within her into a friend.

GETTING TO KNOW OURSELVES

We spend so much time trying to create impressions upon others that we seldom think of trying to know ourselves, to know who we are. At a recent survey among college students it was ascertained that 90 per cent of boys and girls were not satisfied with themselves; they didn't like themselves. I believe a good percentage of us don't like ourselves because we don't know ourselves better, and if we did we all would seek improvement.

Of course I don't mean standing before the mirror in self-adoration and conceit. This would mean going away from ourselves into a world of fantasy and unreality which is negative and unproductive; we must have a goal toward others every day and if the goal is toward ourselves, it should mean self-improvement in relationship to others around us. If we like ourselves as human beings we will be more useful to ourselves. We must realize that we put our self-image behind our face . . . a self-image built as a result of our past successes and failures. If we are fearful and resentful because of past failures and use these negative feelings in our present undertaking, we distrust ourselves, distort our self-image. We are ashamed of this self image, an image we can't live with. We quarrel with ourselves and extend this dissatisfaction to others. Then we put on a mask, boast, and pretend with others in order to bolster up our ego. We then do not like the stranger within us; we like him less than the stranger around us, not realizing that we created this unpalatable stranger ourselves.

If we use the self-confidence of past successes in our present daily undertaking we like ourselves in the proper way because we have not only accepted ourselves for what we are but also for what we can be, and we use courage to enhance our self-image.

If we know this we will realize that our self-image is built on successes and failures and if we forget past failures, rise above them, and concentrate on the present success of today, we will suddenly get to know ourselves better, to like ourselves more. This automatically means turning away from anger, resentment, and cruelty and this means we give our better selves to others.

THE HIDDEN STRANGER AT WORK

In the early part of my career I returned to New York after doing postgraduate work in plastic surgery in Europe and became connected with a hospital. After completing the repair of a harelip on a newborn baby one day, I noticed on the operative schedule that another surgeon was booked to reconstruct the depressed nose of a young girl with a cartilage graft taken from the rib. I went into the amphitheater with a student I was teaching, to watch.

The surgeon, who was about to shape the cartilage graft to proper size before inserting it into the nose, was angry and resentful at my appearance. He turned his back on me and continued to shape the cartilage hidden from view. The student and I were stunned at his behavior.

I recalled that only a year before, I bad completed mv course in plastic surgery in Berlin under Professor Tacqlies Joseph and had gone to London for further study with Sir Harold Gillies, the great British surgeon who did such remarkable work on the wounded soldiers of World War I. Though he was the teacher, be was anxious to learn the surgical techniques I had picked up in Germany, and in return he taught me all his various procedures of skin grafting. We shared our knowledge. But the New York doctor kept his knowledge to himself. He had a distorted image of himself. The stranger within him was his enemy, making him less than he could be, since he refused to impart his knowledge to others. Gillies and I had a self-image we could be proud of. Our hidden stranger was our friend.

Abraham Lincoln once said: "God must have loved the common people; he made so many of them." He was wrong. All of us are uncommon. We are all different . . . yet the same in one respect. We can improve our self-image and learn to like ourselves better—and be happy.

Five minutes a day can change us for the better. We relax for five minutes a day in the room of our mind and as we do, we remember that the stranger within us doesn't have to be a stranger after all. We remember that we have a self-image we put there and, most important, we change this self image, improve it, make it adequate for our needs. We can make this stranger our friend . . . a helpful friend for life, a friend who will put us on the road to happiness!

HOW TO USE THE MIRROR

There is a mirror on the wall in the room of your mind.

1. Look at yourself. Look behind the face. Try to see your inner self . . . the stranger within the heartbeat of your mind.
2. Try to understand this stranger within . . . this self-image, which will change and look different when you are happy and when you are unhappy.
3. This stranger within is your friend when you are confident of your present undertaking because you remember the times you were successful in the past.
4. This stranger within is your enemy when you are overcome with negative feelings that inhibit you . . . feelings of unbelief, indecision, anger, resentment.
5. The face of your self-image will look forever young and happy if you have courage, understanding, self-respect, a sense of direction, and belief that you can be better than you think you are.
6. Most important of all. Our stranger within does not rule us. We rule him! We are only what we want him to be . . . what we want our self-image to be. All we need to remember is our self-respect.
7. Napoleon once said: "None but myself did me any harm." Remember that.

CHAPTER 4

THE HAPPINESS MECHANISM

WHAT IS HAPPINESS? Happiness is a state of mind or habit where we have pleasant thoughts a greater part of the time. It is a built-in mechanism within us. To understand this better it might be well to realize that we also have a built-in worry mechanism. These are not two separate entities like two ears on the face, but they are interlocking processes that work daily in our lives, expressing our emotions, and when we begin to understand who we are, we alone can decide which mechanism we want to use for our purposes because we can control them. We can make a habit of worrying, or of being happy.

Worry like happiness is also a state of mind. Here we throw on the screen of our minds the failures we had in the past and thereby build pictures of failure for some new goal we are undertaking long before we have reached this goal.

We have a forebrain that makes us quite different from the animal. This forebrain situated behind our forehead is the center for our desires, our goals, our hopes. And when we have a goal in view, we call upon the tape recorder of our midbrain that has registered our past experience—good and bad—and depending on what we choose from this tape recorder we will go forward toward this goal either with a happy, winning feeling of confidence or with a negative feeling that we will fail even before we reach this goal.

THE SERVO-MECHANISM AT WORK

In other words, we have a servomechanism in our midbrain which is an electronic machine, an electronic device so small, so compact that it far surpasses any electronic computing mechanism man has ever devised or ever could device—an electronic tape recorder of our experiences that serves us according to what we ask of it.

If in a present undertaking we have positive feelings of well-being as a result of past successes we move toward our goal with confidence.

For example . . . we, as adults, want to pick up a pen on a desk. We do so successfully for the following reason: When we were younger and didn't have the experience of picking up a pen . . . we, say as a child, wanting the pen, picked it up from the table or desk with our band, only after the arm zigzagged in the direction of the pen. After numerous attempts at zigzagging to get the pen, we did it properly without unnecessary motion, so that as adults when we have a desire to take the pen from the desk, the forebrain sends a message to the midbrain which calls upon our tape recorder, which has recorded permanently the successful performance of the act and the midbrain goes about the business of stimulating the numerous muscles involved in the process of picking up the pen. This is done unconsciously since we do not know all the muscles intricately involved in picking up the pen. The desire is in the forebrain. The unconscious performance of the act begins in the midbrain.

Take another example. When as a child we sit at the piano and play we are suddenly told by a parent or else we overhear a parent say that we are clumsy with our hands and that we can never be a pianist. If we believe this, and as children we usually do, we register this negative feeling about our bands in our electronic computing machine or tape recorder, and in the future when we have to use our hands in a subsequent undertaking, we unconsciously recall this negative feeling of the past and we fail in our undertaking with our hands in a delicate performance long before we have tried to reach the goal.

The first successful performance in picking up the pen instills self-confidence, a feeling of well-being and happiness.

The second example at the piano shows that we have and use a negative feeling of the past to fail in an undertaking in the present, to prove to the world that what our parents said about our fingers being clumsy is true. This pattern of negative feeling has, as its base worry, the fear of failure.

Thus the worry mechanism and the happiness mechanism within us are there for the choosing. And we are bound to choose properly to reach our goal of self-fulfillment if we are willing to learn a little more about who we are and how we function as human beings.

THE FUNDAMENTAL EMOTIONS

From the days long, long ago at the dawn of civilization, when our ancestors were savages, four fundamental emotions were developed. They were laughter, weeping, anger, and fear. When two savages met on a plain they fought for survival. Anger thus came into being. The man who overpowered his enemy laughed over his victory. The defeated, injured man changed the anger etched on his face to weeping. And then in the future at another encounter the man who lost would remember his defeat and be filled with fear for the future. And worry is nothing more than an extension of fear, and if this fear was overpowering, our forefathers then learned the emotion of terror.

Those emotions have been registered in the electronic tape recorder in our midbrain and when these emotions are expressed our tape recorder causes certain facial muscles to contract to register these various emotions, depending on whether we succeed or fail. It is these facial muscles which distinguish us so greatly from the animal.

As we sit in the room of our mind we see a picture of a man who has lost heavily in the market. He is mentally depressed. Worry is written on his face; his forehead is furrowed with wrinkles and the corners of his mouth sag . . . sure signs of anxiety, low spirits, and despair.

When we are tormented with fear our brain sends an order to certain muscles of the face to prepare for weeping, as if we were still infants on the verge of screaming. But unconsciously, we can partially check this impulse through will power and habit. The voluntary suppression of crying is reflected on the features by a drooping of the angle of the mouth and by a peculiar furrowing of the forehead, which can be compared to the shape of a horse-shoe. The ancient sculptors were familiar with the latter symbol of grief, for it is clearly demonstrated in the statues of Laocoon and the Arrentino.

Now when we laugh the upper lip is elevated and retracted, causing the wrinkles about the angles of the mouth and about the eyes which are highly characteristic of smiling, happy people.

To conclude:

1. Happiness is a state of mind, a habit. So is worry.
2. Worry produces a frown and a drooping of the angle of the mouth.
3. Happiness means a smile with the angle of the mouth raised.
4. The happiness and worry mechanisms are interlocking processes that work daily in our lives.
5. Remember the words of Plato: "Nothing in the affairs of man is worth worrying about."
6. Our servo-mechanism is built for success and happiness, not for failure.
7. We have the choice of developing the happiness mechanism.
8. We also have the power within us to spread the happiness habit to others.
9. Remember the words of judge Jonah Goldstein: "Happiness is the only product in the world that multiplies by division."

CHAPTER 5

HOW TO BE HAPPY

WE ARE IN THE ROOM OF OUR MIND, and I am recalling an experience I had . . .

I am seated in a car waiting for someone who is shopping in the main street of St. Croix in the Virgin Islands. A man of about fifty-five with a smile on his young face crosses the street, comes over to me, and says:

"Good morning to you, sir."

"Good morning."

"Lovely day."

"Yes. "

"Any vegetables today?"

I say—no and, smiling, he goes back to his oblong box of fruits and vegetables, taking his time of course, for he is lame and he drags his left foot.

A native woman is waiting for him and when he manages to get seated in his chair he says to her: "The man says he doesn't care for any vegetables today. He does no cooking. He must be a bachelor." And now they laugh.

He is dressed in a cheap khaki shirt and trousers and I find out later many facts about him; that all he has in the world is this oblong box of fruits and vegetables with roller skates attached to it underneath in front and wooden handles attached to it in the rear.

At the end of the day when the sun sets, Christensen, for that is the name I have given him, places his chair over the top of the box, lifts the handles, smiles, then travels slowly down the street whistling, soon to disappear from view as he carries what is left of the mangoes, papayas, bananas, beets, cabbages, and other vegetables.

And early next morning he is pushing his handmade cart toward his place in the sun on the main street. And I know it is he even if my eyes are shut, because his whistle and his smile are just as much his trademark as his vegetables. I can hear the whistle distinctly, not too loud, not too soft. It is impossible to describe it. One thing it isn't; it isn't discordant, nor does it indicate fear or concern as if one were bolstering up his courage passing through an empty street at night. No. This whistle has one definite quality, and man, woman, or child detects it with ease. It has the quality that comes with contentment; a quality of joy and happiness that a new sunny day has come upon this tiny island no more than twenty-five miles long, inspiring the aquamarine water to ripple. And what else is inspiring? The smile on his face when I see him at close quarters.

Christensen has been doing this daily for many years. None of the natives know exactly bow long, for they are so used to it: he being part of the community as a clock is of a tower. The khaki outfit is the only attire he uses during the week—a trademark, like his smile, his whistle, his vegetables. But now it is Sunday—the day he puts his cart of vegetables to rest. Here, early in the morning, he is walking down the street dressed in a starched and pressed linen suit as clean as a fleecy white cloud. And with him is his wife, dressed in white, walking slowly to keep in step with his limp. And soon they get up on the sidewalk and disappear into the church. Then, when services are over, be is on the street again whistling as usual with that smile on his young face as he creeps homeward, not ever dreaming that the church bells might be applauding him for his humility and simplicity, and for being happy, and perhaps inspiring others to be happy too.

Christensen had found how to enjoy life; bow to be happy. It was simple to him in his own simple way. And it can be simple to all of us in our own way wherever we are; we don't need any tropical island to achieve it. All we have to do is take five minutes off during the day when we sit in the room of our mind, learn a little about ourselves, and teach ourselves the habit Christensen learned, the habit Christensen practiced.

THE HAPPINESS MECHANISM AT WORK

What do we learn from Christensen? The working of the happiness mechanism, the habit of happiness.

What are the ingredients that went to make up the state of happiness in Christensen?

1. He smiled many times a day. It became as natural to him as breathing air.
2. He was cheerful . . . as cheerful as anyone could possibly be.
3. He was friendly toward other people. He was part of humanity.
4. He was less critical and more tolerant and understanding of other people.
5. He was successful in his own undertaking. Success in his little field was inevitable. And be himself made of himself a personality that was successful, the personality he wanted to be.
6. He did not let his own opinion color facts in a negative way. What do I mean? I mean this: He had an unhappy past; his crippled leg indicates that. He must have been filled with frustration and despair in the past, but he learned that be must not look back to the past, but live for the day in hand, that every day is a composite life that has to be lived now without letting the despair of the past distort it and keep him from his goal of having a happy day.
7. Knowing this, be learned to react as calmly and intelligently as possible to the day, no matter what happened.
8. He knew he could do nothing about his crippled leg, or

about other existing negative facts. He closed his mind to it, not like an ostrich digging its head into sand . . . but with intelligence refusing to let negative feelings, worry and the like, throttle him for the completion of a happy day.

THE UNHAPPINESS MECHANISM

We also have an unhappiness mechanism . . . the habit of unhappiness that comes from constant worry, constant fear, constant negative feelings we invoke from the past in an undertaking of the present. This we will discuss in detail later. At present it will be worth our while to understand the ingredients that express the state of unhappiness.

1. A frown on the face instead of a smile.
2. Sad instead of cheerful.
3. Not friendly to others.
4. Critical of others. Less tolerant and understanding.
5. Not successful in understanding the personality we don't want to be.
6. Letting our own opinion color facts in a negative way.
7. Not having learned to react calmly to things every day.
8. Living on negative feelings of the past and present.

WORRY SHOULD BE A CHALLENGE

We all worry. But worry should be a challenge to stand up to our full stature of dignity. Stress is part of living and we must learn to cope with it, not let it destroy us. We never solve anything by carrying worry from business to our home then to our bed. We must learn that when we do this we burden ourselves with the extra unnecessary tensions that pile on our backs and weigh us down, making us less than what we are, making us walk away from ourselves, making us become the small potatoes we actually aren't.

There are other extra unnecessary stresses that create extra unnecessary tensions that make us less than we are, but we will come to this later, and we will understand them for what they are and we will learn how to cope with them. And when we do, it will be easier to understand the happiness mechanism that seeks to make us successful as human beings if we will only give ourselves the chance.

It is up to us to make it a practice for five minutes every day to have pleasant ideas and memories, those fine feelings of usefulness and kindness that make us part of mankind. We must make a habit of this as we would of breathing exercises every day. Habits are responses which we have learned to perform automatically without having to "think," like tying a shoelace in the morning or brushing our teeth. And it is just as easy to have the happiness habit as the unhappiness habit. The choice is ours.

HOW WE FUNCTION BEST

1. Since we are goal-striving beings, we function best when we are striving for some useful goal.
2. And we express happiness in the achievement of this goal.
3. Happiness can be and should be a goal in itself like breakfast in the morning, and we should strive for it aggressively as we would to get food for sustenance.
4. Deliberately seeing the difference between the happiness habit and the unhappiness syndrome is more than a palliative. It has practical value because we should always remember we are built for success and it is our right to choose what is best for us, and the happiness habit is best for us . . . a mental habit we can cultivate without ever imposing on others.
5. We must also remember the obvious. We cannot be happy all the time. Problems beset us every day. Why

make them worse with increased fears, inferiority, resentment, uncertainty, that prevent us from achieving our goal?

6. Review each of the eight ingredients of happiness and unhappiness. See how unhappiness destroys self-esteem. Perhaps we will then realize that we have no right to let it push us around. We must stand up to it, refusing to be a slave to it. We owe it to our own stature of dignity.

7. We must understand once and for all that happiness is not something that is earned or deserved. There is no morality involved here any more than in breathing . . . any more than in survival. And it is not a reward for being unselfish.

8. The act of unhappiness is selfish in that it destroys our worth.

9. The act of happiness in a special moral sense is unselfish in that in making us what we can be, we automatically become more understanding and therefore less unselfish to our fellow man.

10. We must think of unhappiness as painful and evil simply because it makes us less than we are.

11. Happiness on the other hand makes us rise to what we really can be.

12. Remember the words of Robert Louis Stevenson: "To be what we are, and to become what we are capable of becoming, is the only end of life."

CHAPTER 6

HOW TO BREAK THE UNHAPPINESS HABIT

I HAVE A PERSONAL CONFESSION TO MAKE, but first, before telling the whole story, I must set the stage in the room of your mind so that you will be able to appreciate it in all its details.

Every hospital operating room has a doctors' dressing room attached to it. When the doctor arrives here to prepare for the operation he is scheduled to perform, he takes off his street clothes and hangs them up in a locker, keeping on only his shoes and socks. Then he dons the operating clothes—his working uniform. These are the white, green, or blue, sterile baggy garments that have been made familiar in so many motion pictures and TV shows about the "men in white," the operating surgeons.

After changing his clothes as I have described, the doctor scrubs his bands and arms with special liquid antiseptic soap and hot water for ten minutes. Drying hands and arms with sterile towels, he then puts on the rubber operating gloves—and, finally, is ready for the operating room and the patient awaiting him.

I suppose every surgeon has a special little routine he has developed over the years in going through this process of changing from street clothes into operating clothes. I know that I have mine. I have never told it to anyone before, not even to members of my family.

Generally I get to the doctors' dressing room of the hospital where I operate at about 7:45 in the morning. Because I like to schedule my first operation of the day as early as possible, I am usually the only doctor using the dressing room at that hour. I take off my street clothes piece by piece the jacket, trousers, shirt, and tie and so on—and hang them up in a locker. (I must point out, in justice to myself, that these lockers, though called lockers, have no locks on them.) So there I am, quite naked except for my shoes and socks.

Now I reach into the right pocket of my trousers with my right hand and pull out whatever money I happened to take with me from home that morning. I roll the bills into a tight wad. Then I lift my left foot up onto a chair and quickly stuff the wad of bills into my left sock.

I close the door of the locker, put on the operating clothes, scrub up at the basin—and am ready for work.

Heaven knows how and when this habit of stuffing my money into my left sock first started—because, for as long as I can remember, I have been literally unconscious of doing it. I daresay, though, that I must have started the practice way, way back—thirty years and more back—when I was a young intern and was preparing for my first experience of assisting at the operating table. I was very poor, as most interns are, and I simply could not risk losing so much as a penny out of the tiny little hoard I kept in my trousers pocket. And so, while taking off my regular clothes and hanging them up, I must have cast about desperately in my mind for some place where the money would be safe. And my eye must have fallen on my sock!

Well, whether or not that was the case, the habit has been ingrained in me for years—for so long, as I have said, that I did not even realize it was a habit.

Then one morning not long ago another doctor happened to get to the doctors' dressing room at the same time I did. And it just so happened, too, that he is a doctor I know very well, whose first name is Paul.

We got undressed together. Then I became aware that Paul was staring at me.

"For the Lord's sake, Mac," he said, "whatever are you doing?"

"What am I doing?" I repeated. "Why, I—"

I looked around. I was quite naked, and my left foot was up on a chair, and I realized that I had just stuffed my roll of bills into my left sock.

"Why," I said, "I'm-I'm-well, you see, I'm just putting my money away in a-well, in a safe place."

"Oh," Paul said, "I see." He turned his head around quickly and seemed to be having difficulty controlling himself, for I heard what sounded suspiciously like a chuckle.

Then I reflected that perhaps it was a little foolish for a grown man to be hiding his money in his sock! So I determined to stop the practice.

Easier said than done! Much, much easier! For the next day when I returned to my office, lo and behold, there my money was in my left sock, as it always was after I came back from the operating room.

Now, I told myself, you said you were going to stop this, so go ahead, stop.

No use. The money was in the left sock again on the following day.

I put the money into the inside pocket of my jacket and pinned it there. To no avail. Habit was too strong. Without really realizing I was doing it, I took the pin out and put the money in the left sock, as always.

Nothing seemed to help.

Then was the habit so strong that I simply could not break it?

Apparently so, for day after day I went on putting the bills into my left sock. The habit had me licked. I despaired of ever changing it.

THE MIRROR

And then I had an idea.

I stopped in at a certain neighborhood shop the next day and the following morning I came to the doctors' dressing room with a long brown package under my arm. I took the brown wrapping paper off—and there revealed was a Mirror about three and a half feet long.

The mirror fitted exactly inside the door of my locker. I left the door open and watched myself in the mirror as I got undressed. jacket, trousers, shirt, tie, underwear.

And now—

Yes, there I was, doing it! Taking the money out of my trousers pocket and stuffing it into my left sock!

The image of the man in the mirror—me—taking the money from my pocket and stuffing it into my sock was so ridiculous, so absolutely absurd, so childish, that I burst out laughing at myself.

I could understand now why Paul had had to turn his head away to hide his mirth.

Yes, I looked ridiculous

And, in laughing at myself, looking at that absurd picture in the mirror, I somehow knew that I had broken the habit for good.

In the following days, that turned out to be exactly the case. The mirror bad done the trick.

BREAKING A HABIT—THE PROBLEM AND THE ANSWER

Bad habits offer one of life's most annoying problems. I think it is safe to say that almost every one of us has some habit or other that he wishes he could get rid of. Some, of course, have more than one habit they would like to lose. Every one of these habits is a problem in itself.

The problem consists in just this: How to destroy the unwanted habit as painlessly and quickly as possible.

Can the problem be solved? It can indeed.

The therapy I as a doctor recommend for solution of the habit problem is, in its essentials, simplicity itself. And by utilizing this simple therapy, anyone who is habit-ridden will find himself freed for all the manifold activities that make life vital and joyful—activities that a destructive habit simply does not leave time for.

To solve the habit problem, it is not necessary, as I did, to buy a mirror and bang it up in front of the place where you are indulging yourself in the habit.

But it is necessary to put up a mental mirror in front of yourself . . . in the room of your mind!

The image you will see there is yourself as other people see you. As the world sees you.

Study that image carefully. Watch it during one entire day. Look at it without sympathy or favor but quite objectively—for that is how the world looks at you.

Now, are there any minutes of the day when you have reason to be proud of the image's behavior? Yes, of course there are.

But are there any minutes of the day when you have reason to be humiliated by the image's behavior? Or. to coin a word, let us say unproud of its behavior?

Yes, alas, there are these minutes too.

And most of the time these minutes you are ashamed of are the ones you are devoting to a foolish, childish, timewasting, or health—destroying habit.

You are looking at yourself now as the world sees you. And of course you wish the world to see you at your best.

You do not wish to look foolish, childish, or weak-willed.

There is only one way to avoid that. End the habit. Look into that mental mirror when the habit next gets its grip on you like an Old Man of the Sea. And of course, I mean that common habit of ours . . . the unhappiness habit, distorted by its *eight repulsive ingredients*.

The mirror makes an ugly sight.

How much better—and how easy—to make it a sight that will please the eyes Instead! We substitute the happiness habit as we visualize the eight attractive ingredients of the happiness mechanism.

And mark my word!—You will find, just as I found with my mirror, that the habit of unhappiness almost magically has gone.

To help you break the unhappiness habit remember the words of James Russell Lowell: "The misfortunes hardest to bear are those which never come."

CHAPTER 7

DEFORMED FACES - DEFORMED IMAGES

Beauty is a gift of God.
—ARISTOTLE

AS A PLASTIC SURGEON who has operated on thousands of people with deformed faces in the past thirty years, I have become a specialist not only in scarred faces but in scarred images. And through this experience of removing disfigurements and the unhappiness that goes with them I have learned a great deal about the destructive emotions of unhappiness that we are all heir to, even if our faces are normal. So that I may impart this knowledge in effective terms I suggest that we now sit in the room of our mind as I talk to you.

We see a child, a girl six months old who has a deformity of the upper lip. She was born with a hole in the center of the upper lip, known as a harelip. She looks like a monstrosity, particularly when she cries. We see the agony in the mother's face as she tries to feed the child.

Now we see her at the age of eight. Her playmates call her "dog face" and she avoids them as much as possible. She blushes whenever they stare at her. She is shy and backward in her schoolwork. She stutters and hisses when she talks and her sentences are choppy and incoherent, as if they too were deformed and subject to the critical scrutiny of her classmates.

We see her now in her teens trying her best to win honors

in her studies to compensate for her deformity, and she does, but she has few friends. She is still uncertain; she still feels inferior. She goes to a school dance and sits alone, unhappy while she watches happy boys and girls dancing.

She is now an adult and we see her get into a bus to go to work. Some people stare at her. Others turn their backs to her. One woman moves away from her, fearful that she may become contaminated. And now we see our main character as a bookkeeper in an office hidden from view behind a cage. What else do we see? Do we see fear, uncertainty, inferiority in her as she does her daily chores? The answer is yes. Do we see resentment, loneliness, emptiness? We do. Do we see unhappiness? There is no doubt about it simply because all these destructive emotions, one by one, have a common characteristic . unhappiness.

What else do we see? We see a young lady, a failure as a human being, even though she works to survive. One thing we don't see is her inner image, the image of her inner face. But as you know, it's there because we all have an inner image of ourselves and in her case this self-image is also disfigured.

And thus, through her, we realize how a deformity affects the behavior and life of a child, an adolescent, an adult Now through a magic scalpel in the hands of a plastic surgeon her lip is corrected and made normal while she is still an infant, long before she is aware of her condition. Now that her lip is normal she goes to school as a normal child and reaches the threshold of adolescence like all other children, and later we see her dancing with a young man who takes her home subsequently, then kisses her before he leaves. They are both happy.

WE TAKE OUR FACES FOR GRANTED

Most of us take our faces for granted. We seldom stop to ponder the very obvious fact that the face is the first thing we look at when meeting a stranger. In conversation we watch our companion's face, either as he speaks or as his expressions register his reactions to the speech of others. Almost as much meaning may be conveyed silently by expression as by the spoken word.

We are extremely face-conscious and, justly or unjustly, use the face as the index to a person's character.

All of us want to be normal, for normality predicates a rational adjustment to the fundamentals of life which, in turn, brings happiness. We cannot be blamed for our faces, but society in general expects and demands normal appearance, and its requirements tend to force the abnormal individual into a personality not necessarily his own. Alfred Adler, in his work on human behavior, has discussed at length the reasons both for society's demands and for the individual's response to these demands. Man, he points out, is physically inferior to all other forms of animal life, and to survive has bad to accept group existence with its benefits and demands. The group offers security and demands conformity.

THE CHILD

Our complete helplessness in infancy makes conformity or non-conformity alike impossible, but very early in childhood we must start making adjustments to the demands of organized society and try to achieve security through standardization. This becomes increasingly complicated as our interests carry us beyond the indulgence of the family circle. Soon we are making concessions and adjustments to the three fundamental problems of adult life—society, sex, and economics.

To outgrow our childish dependence, to assume our proper place in the group, and to participate, therefore, in the feeling of group security—all these are phases of one process, which must be completed successfully if we are to wrest any happiness from life. If, for any reason, through circumstances or our own inadequacy, such as a facial disfigurement, our fellows do not admit us into full brotherhood, we are denied that precious sense of security.

Children, being too inexperienced to feel compassion,

thoughtlessly shun those who cannot keep up with the crowd. They openly criticize or ridicule abnormal appearance. Their naiveté' can be cruel as well as charming. The disfigured child cannot escape their attacks. In proportion to the severity of his defect and his sensitiveness, he will find compensation in some way for his loss of security and for the feeling that he is, more or less, an outcast. He may become an introvert and a recluse, recessive and passively antagonistic to society. On the other hand he may react violently and become a bully, trying to force his personality on his fellows and to get even with a world that does not want to accept him as it does normal people.

THE ADOLESCENT

Adolescence is the age of rapid growth, and awkwardness, when the secondary sex characteristics appear. As the face grows, the features become more prominent, and any irregularity in facial topography is embarrassingly emphasized. An abnormal nose, only mildly noticeable during childhood becomes increasingly disfiguring up to the age of seventeen, when the nasal tissues cease growing. Protruding ears flanking a thick oval face become grotesque. Birthmarks grow as the face matures. Similarly, the receding chin, the pendulous lip, and other blemishes assume tragic proportions.

In normal children the age of adolescence is marked by an attempt to outgrow an inferior position in society. They enter the struggle on equal terms with others of their own age, but children with facial handicaps are not even granted that much security. If their disfigurements set them apart in childhood, their burdens now become doubly heavy. It is not unusual for such people to carry into adult life acute feelings of inferiority, typified by either extremely retiring or obnoxiously domineering dispositions. They are always uncomfortable, always unhappy, seldom adjusted to the world.

If a facially abnormal individual is ashamed of his deformity he will blush easily when stared at and, of course, he will be stared at more than a normal person. In his attempt to minimize the disfigurement he will try to assume positions which hide it. Morbidly sensitive people shun their fellows or, if obliged to associate with others, stammer and make pointless, inappropriate remarks. Energy which should go into constructive work is diverted into hopeless brooding and usually futile efforts at compensation. Constant mental turmoil, worry, and fear will finally exhaust the individual's psychic reserve and give rise to a neurosis which is essentially a fatigue manifestation brought about by the dissipation of physical or psychic capital. Such a neurosis, beginning insidiously in adolescence, may erupt violently during adulthood at the least expected time, when the individual is unprepared to wrestle with sudden emergencies.

A physical handicap, great or small, which deeply affects the individual's frame of mind, can, in turn, irritate and upset the various organs of the body, influencing also disposition and behavior. Those individuals who compensate aggressively for their deformities place undue emphasis on egotism and become morbidly intent on their efforts to attain distinction and to force their way into an unreceptive society. If the individual has a forceful enough personality, be may achieve a certain degree of security and fulfill certain obligations toward society, but he cannot attain real happiness. The fact remains that he still is facially abnormal. Strangers will continue to stare at him, and all his compensatory efforts tend only to make him more conscious of his physical inferiority.

THE ADULT

The adult with a facial blemish, carried since childhood or acquired suddenly by accident, is subject to the same penalties as the adolescent. If he has lived with his disfigurement for some time he has either achieved an unhappy balance by many concessions made to society without concomitant benefits, or he is completely at odds with his fellow men. If be has acquired the disfigurement accidentally, be is suddenly confronted with new problems of association, sex, and occupation.

Of course, many people are not at all affected by their deformity. A good number succeed in living independently, their egos sturdy enough to ignore expressed or implied criticism. Yet even these comparatively thick-skinned few may suffer when swayed by the greatest of human emotions, love, for sexual attraction is inextricably, inevitably bound up with what we are pleased to call beauty. Beauty plays a stellar role in the duel of the sexes, and rare, indeed, is the passion which deigns to favor deformity. It is poignantly, tragically true that ugliness is not loved.

Such handicaps as have been mentioned not only cause personal unhappiness in varying degrees, but often constitute insurmountable economic as well as social barriers. The seriously deformed cannot secure work. Neuroses develop in others. They are unable to work efficiently and to hold jobs. Still others are forced to do menial tasks for which they are congenitally unfit. The unhappy effects of such conditions are visited not only upon the afflicted individual, but upon his family and dependents as well.

The livelihood of many people, is, in a large measure, dependent upon their appearance. Actors, musicians, salesmen, teachers, and other professionals are greatly handicapped by any facial deformity obvious to the audience whose approval signifies economic security.

BEAUTY AND UGLINESS

We cannot change society. People will always react in the same way to beauty and ugliness as long as the race exists. Hundreds of books have been written about beauty, but our libraries contain no works on ugliness, although it is far more common than beauty, as the faces in any crowd prove conclusively. A lovely or handsome, even a merely normal, face is a splendid asset, but its owner is seldom conscious of the fact, though she or he may reap daily the benefits of attractiveness. The individual with ugly, abnormal features cannot forget his own repellent appearance. Society will not let him. Few people can overlook a physical blemish in someone to whom they are talking. Personal relationships are thrown out of gear by self-consciousness based on deformity, which eventually becomes a cancer in the personality of the afflicted one.

Even the most common forms of ugliness, trifling as they may seem to the superficial observer, have a more serious effect on personality than most of us realize. The man or woman who has to carry around a deformity twenty-four hours a day, knowing all the time that his associates are conscious of it and repelled by his defect, however slight, is made utterly wretched.

If a man's ears are much larger than the average, we consider them funny as well as ugly. An excessively long nose seems ridiculous, and various other deformities inspire laughter. There is cruelty in so much of our humor that psychologists have been led to conclude that laughter is often merely an expression of contempt—a malicious comment on our fellow men in distress. Fear, anger, disgust, and laughter are all expressed by essentially the same muscles and are probably closely related emotions. When we jeer at the grotesque clowns in the circus, it is very likely that we are expressing, in a mild form, the revulsion we feel when looking at hideously scarred war veterans. Mingled with this is a rather smug feeling of satisfaction that we are not as ridiculous as Cyrano or as ugly as Caliban and are nearer the norm than they are. It is desirable to approximate the norm, of course, but we seldom realize that Cyrano and Caliban also thought it desirable and yearned after it with a desperation we can never fully comprehend.

Few individuals whose appearance seems comical to us are equipped emotionally to clown their way through life, but the adaptable minority turn their deformity into a valuable economic asset. Most clownish-looking people, however, want merely to be average folk, and are unwilling to be forced into roles which they are unable to play. The plight of the comedian with the broken heart has appealed to nearly every great writer. It constitutes one of life's most poignant tragedies.

It is not vanity which makes a pleasing visage of such vital importance to us. A normal appearance eliminates a torturing feeling of inferiority and a distorted view of the world. It obviates that terrific outlay of energy needed to offset a physical defect. Physical appearance and mental reactions, as we have seen, are closely joined from earliest childhood. To look one's best is to be mentally at one's best.

We have seen at the beginning of this chapter how the self-image of a child is distorted if she has a harelip and how the self-image is brought back to normal when the harelip is repaired, bringing with it the right to happiness. What about the disfigured inner self-image behind a normal face?

CHAPTER 8

THE SELF-IMAGE BEHIND THE NORMAL FACE

A S I HAVE PREVIOUSLY MENTIONED, each of us carries a mental picture of himself that is not visible when we see ourselves in the mirror. This self image is behind the face even though we may not see it. It is our own idea of what we are, derived from our beliefs about ourselves formed by our past experiences. In this respect we mentally become our own plastic surgeon and build our own self-image. If we build our self-image from past successes we have a self-image that makes us happy. If we build our self-image from past failures we scar our inner image with our own hands, and since we are ashamed of this self-image, we are unhappy only because our personality and behavior come from our self-image.

CREATING A NEW SELF-IMAGE

Fortunately we can change our self-image regardless of age, which means we can start to live a new life if we want to. We can become our own plastic surgeon and remove the scar of unhappiness deep within our self-image and make happiness our goal. If we have an unhappy self-image we will automatically do things to prove we are unhappy. If on the other hand our self-image is one of happiness we'll go about our business to prove that this is so. We can't think positively about negative beliefs any more than we can think negatively about constructive beliefs.

As a plastic surgeon I've been asked many times where the connection lies between surgery and psychology. This I explained in the previous chapter by showing that a person with an outer scar has an inner scar as well. A person with an outer scar is affected by it psychologically, socially, or economically, which produces this inner scar which in turn sets up the various negative feelings and distortions mentioned in this previous chapter.

Thus removing the outer scar eradicates the inner scar simultaneously and the individual becomes someone else. He becomes his true self. He goes away from his inner self to the outside world where he belongs as part of reality to reach a goal that will bring him peace of mind and happiness. But there are exceptions to this in a small percentage of cases. All plastic surgeons have had the experience of removing a facial scar or deformity with unusual skill only to find the patient saying that the surgery made no difference—that he looks the same. Showing him the photographs taken before the surgery, which reveal the deformity, and those showing the dramatic change brought about by the surgery, does little good. He will say perhaps that the scar isn't noticeable but it is still there and that be feels the same as before.

Of course to a child born with a congenital defect like a harelip, mentioned in the previous chapter, plastic reconstructive surgery can really perform miracles by bringing a newfound happiness with a newfound normal face. From this it would be quite easy to surmise that people with normal faces should have no psychological problems should be cheerful and happy—but we know that this is far from the truth.

THE INNER SCAR

Less than one-tenth of one per cent of the population have a facial disfigurement as the result of a birth defect or of , an accident at home, on the highway, or in industry, and these people seek the aid of the plastic surgeon. But 90 per cent of the population with normal faces who would never dream of plastic surgery have an inner scar arising from negative feelings of inferiority, from fear, uncertainty, resentment, loneliness, and emptiness . . . an inner scar on their self-image that they put there themselves, and then suffer the inner tensions and corrosions mentioned in the previous chapter as if they had an outer scar. Of course the inner scar is far more serious simply because we are not aware of it.

Let us imagine for a moment that, as we sit in the room of our mind, we see a beautiful woman fixing her hair before the mirror. Her features are lovely and there is not a mark on her skin. But despite her beauty she is unhappy. You see it in her droopy look and the frown on her forehead . . . and in her eyes. The image of herself behind the face is distorted by resentment—yet she is not aware of it. What is her resentment? She hates a club woman who has a better command of the English language and who has intrigued a mutual friend, a business executive. The face of her image within is scarred; the body of her inner image is slouched as if she were carrying the weight of the world on her shoulders. The hands of her inner image are clenched in a spasm of futility. Yet this woman could look as attractive within as without if she only knew what resentment was doing to her. Later we will show how she can be her true self and remove that inner scar that shouldn't be there in the first place, because she wasn't born with it, and, like all of us, has a right to be herself.

Now we see a man in front of the mirror, shaving. He is handsome but looks troubled. He has an inner scar from fear. He is worried about a new undertaking. He is in a spasm of doubt, and the only thing be is certain about, even before he tries, is that he will fail.

He is an insurance salesman but he is fearful of making a mistake. He is one of the men who will speak to a group of colleagues telling of his recent experience in his field. He remembers that a month ago when he was out of town he was called upon to speak. He got up . . . felt panicky because he thought he might make a mistake and lose the respect of his listeners. He couldn't speak. He sat down certain that he would faint.

He too can remove his inner sear if he understands who he really is, and this he can do with the rest of us, as we will demonstrate later in the book, by forgetting the past which inhibited him, by thinking only of his present goal, by having courage and confidence in himself because he knows his subject, and because he knows that he has a right to be better than what he thought he was, that he has a right to be his true self.

If we are to be reasonably happy we must know our self-image and this we can do because there is no magic or deep secret to it. We must develop a self-image we can live with, a self-image acceptable to ourselves, a self image we like, trust, and believe in. If we are proud of this self-image we function best. If on the other hand our self-image is an object of shame we attempt to hide it rather than express it. Creative expression is blocked. We become hostile . . . someone we really aren't. We walk away from reality and the goal of happiness we are entitled to.

Remember these key points:

1. We are our own plastic surgeon and build our own self-image.
2. If we build a self-image from past successes, we have a self-image that makes us happy.
3. If we build a self-image from past failures, we distort our self-image. This produces unhappiness.
4. We can't think positively about negative beliefs; we can't think negatively about constructive beliefs.
5. Regardless of age we can change our self-image and start a new life.
6. We must develop a self-image we can live with, a self-image we can trust and believe in. In that way we function best.
7. If we are ashamed of our self-image we become less than we really are, blocking creative expression.
8. Can we really change our self-image? Can we really

change from unhappiness to happiness? We can, definitely, by using our imagination.

9. It is well to remember the words of Henry David Thoreau: "What a man thinks of himself, that it is which determines, or rather indicates, his fate."

CHAPTER 9

THE POWER OF THE IMAGINATION

NOW WE SEE IN THE ROOM OF OUR MIND a young man in his early twenties. He is a second-year medical student. He is slim, has bushy brown hair, hazel eyes, and a small mustache to give the impression that he is older and a full-fledged doctor. He is seated behind his desk in a classroom of about sixty students. They are all listening to a man —a teacher in his late forties who has a walrus mustache and wears a long white coat that ends near his ankles. He stands in front of the class near his desk and blackboard. His name is Doctor Dappenheimer. He is lecturing on some aspect of pathology and when he is through he calls upon the young man with the bushy brown hair, hazel eyes, and small mustache to stand up.

This young man's face was calm while taking notes and now suddenly he looks flustered as he stands up . . . knowing this is an oral quiz. He is worried and agitated even before he has heard the question on pathology. He knows his subject but be is overcome with a spasm of fright when he gets up. He is shy and hates the stare of the other students. He hears the question and be can't answer properly. He sits down, then wonders why he didn't answer the question properly, because he knew the answer, but somehow it didn't come out of him. He is unhappy, dejected. How do I know all this about this young man? Well, I was this young man!

This happened many times at the beginning of the semester and suddenly I was paralyzed with the thought that I would flunk the course and I would never reach the goal of being a doctor . . . a goal that was my whole life.

Now we watch this same man again in the same class but in this instance the students are writing answers to questions during a written examination. The young man is calm, confident as he looks through the microscope at the slide and writes on paper what the condition is, what the prognosis is. He is relaxed. The students are not watching him as they do when he stands up during an oral quiz. He has no negative feelings. Fear doesn't inhibit him. His answers are accurate, to the point, and he gets A for his efforts.

Yet he dreads the thought of a future oral quiz. He worries he may flunk the course. He remembers his desperate desire to be a doctor and through it he suddenly gets an idea. He says to himself: "The next time this so-and-so Dappenheimer quizzes me orally I'll stand up but I'll think I'm looking through a microscope at a slide and I will answer the question as if I were writing it down on paper and not seeing the face of the so-and-so Dappenheimer and all the faces of those pupils." And to his surprise and to the surprise of all he is coherent, logical, and answers brilliantly without hesitation. And the one who is most surprised is the so-and-so Dappenheimer.

Now we see this young man in cap and gown graduating from the school of medicine. He is a full-fledged doctor and he has a smile of happiness on his face.

THE IMAGINATION AT WORK

What happened when I was this second-year medical student? I was the product of my imagination, plus and minus. When I stood up to answer a question I was shy and fearful of talking before an audience. I used my imagination destructively by not thinking of the answer to the question but in worrying about how I looked to the students. My imagination led me astray from my goal and I suddenly became someone else even though I knew the answer. I was flustered long before the question was asked. I had a mental picture of failure on the screen of my mind before I even started. I was myself, on the other hand, calm and relaxed, during the written examination. I had the picture of success on the screen of my mind. I thought of my goal, nothing else, and answered the question properly.

In both instances I used imagination, destructively on one hand, constructively on the other. This only proves how powerful the force of the imagination is in our daily lives, whoever we may be, or whatever goal we may have in mind.

We use our imagination positively or negatively, depending on what image we have of ourselves. We always act, feel, and perform in accordance with what we imagine to be true about ourselves and our environment.

IMAGINATION IS A HABIT

Reality is nothing more than imagination put to use. Negative imagination produces negative habits and negative results. Positive imagination produces positive habits and positive results. I turned a crisis into an opportunity when I realized as a student that I would never be a doctor if I flunked the course in pathology. Knowing my goal and not losing sight of it, I put my imagination to constructive, worthwhile use and succeeded in changing failure into success. If I could, when I did not know what maturity and experience were, so can the rest of us.

We use our imagination every day of our lives. Here are a few examples. We see a woman who plans a party and is about to bake a cake . . . a man who goes to sell an article to a customer . . . a doctor who is treating a patient . . . four women who are playing bridge . . . a man who is playing golf.

In these instances we invoke the images of past successes to help us in our present undertaking which will bring happiness. On the other band we see a frightened salesman wondering how be will handle a customer before he sees him . . . or a doubtful or worried man at the golf course, or a worried basketball or baseball player. These individuals call upon the images of the past failures which jam their own opportunities of doing the job successfully because they think of failure.

We must have a proper image of ourselves: be ourselves, be what we are instead of trying to be someone else!

CREATIVE ROLE-PLAYING

Now imagine a man throwing a basketball into the basket, a woman putting a golf ball into the hole, a boxer shadowboxing before a bout, and, finally, a salesman selling an insurance policy to a customer.

Each in his mind played a game with his imagination before the undertaking. Each recalled how he did it successfully in the past and be used this experience with confidence for the present goal. As a matter of fact this book tip till now has been about the use and abuse of the imagination.

Let us see again the insurance salesman selling an insurance policy to a customer. He is the same man of the previous chapter who dreaded to speak before an audience of his colleagues. I told him of my own experience in Doctor Dappenheimer's class. He got the idea of playing a role—of imagining he was successful selling insurance to a client when he got up to talk to a group of people. He turned a crisis into an opportunity and it wasn't long before be became an excellent speaker. He rose above his fear. He found himself; he found the truth about himself.

As a matter of fact successful men and women always play roles in their mind . . . use mental pictures and rehearsal practice to achieve success and happiness.

Action is the product of the imagination. Habit is the result of imagination. Happiness and unhappiness are two daily products of the imagination. We can achieve either one with our imagination, which opens the door to our living less life or more life. It is up to us. We are only what we think we are, what we imagine we are! And thus imagination is the heart of our emotional being, the heart of our existence. And finally we must remember that the imagination is not the gift of the few, the inventor, the poet, the creator. We are our own inventors, creators, poets who without a word go about the business of living every day. So let us live in happiness.

WHAT IS PSYCHO-CYBERNETICS?

The science of psycho-cybernetics regards the midbrain as an automatic goal-seeking machine, a servo-mechanism which steers its way to a goal by use of stored information in the midbrain. This does not mean that we are a machine but that we have the world's most remarkable electronic computer of our experience in the midbrain, which we control and operate through our forebrain behind our forehead which is the seat of our desires and goals. When we have a desire for happiness we put our servomechanism to work, to work toward happiness.

Since our feelings and behavior depend on our images we can practice the happiness habit because our nervous system cannot tell the difference between an actual experience or one that is vividly imagined. And we get a good mental picture of happiness by recalling happy moments of the past. Practice will make perfect since by this sort of role-playing, repeated, we induce our forebrain to have a desire, a goal for happiness, and this, being a persistent goal, will set the midbrain to recall the past successes to make us happy in the present undertaking.

Thus the creative servomechanism within us can help us find our best self if our "happiness self" is the picture we want, a picture in which we play the leading role. This in essence brings about a change in personality. However, this doesn't mean we must create a fictitious, unreal self, arrogant, powerful egotistic. We must find our "real self" and part of our "real self" is the happiness habit that belongs to all of us. We must neither overrate nor underrate ourselves in the acquisition of this happiness habit. We must remember we were put on this earth to succeed, not fail. So, in the room of our mind we must practice for a moment every day—exercise our imagination productively, making a habit of it which will build new memories for us, store them for the future in our midbrain. Positive memories will bring positive responses just as negative memories bring negative responses. And finally, in the acquisition of our daily goal we must not be afraid of making a mistake, nor permit a mistake to inhibit us from accomplishing a future goal.

We remember the following when we sit in the room of our mind.

1. We use our imagination positively or negatively every day of our lives.
2. Reality is imagination put to work.
3. Negative imagination produces negative habits, negative results. Positive imagination produces positive habits, positive results.
4. We turn a crisis into an opportunity by invoking images of past successes to help us in our present undertaking.
5. Recalling past failures brings present failures.
6. Abusing our imagination makes us what we really aren't.
7. We play a successful role in the room of our mind to give us confidence before tackling a problem.
8. Happiness and unhappiness are the result of creative and destructive imagination. We are therefore what we think we are.
9. We can live in happiness by remembering my principle of psychocybemetics, which means that we are born with a servo-mechanism to succeed provided we have a goal, and provided our goal is a useful, happy one.
10. We must not overrate or underrate ourselves in the acquisition of the happiness habit. We accept ourselves for what we are and do not try to imitate someone else when we try to reach our daily goal.
11. Remember the words of Ralph Waldo Emerson: "Imagination is not the talent of some men but is the health of every man."

CHAPTER 10

ARE WE HYPNOTIZED?

THE PROPER USE OF THE IMAGINATION can be equivalent to the beginning of a goal and a belief in this goal. And if this belief is strong enough we hypnotize ourselves with it. All our habits, good or bad, are in a measure the product of daily self-hypnosis when we perform habits automatically like brushing our teeth in the morning, or having breakfast.

We are now in the room of our mind looking at an elderly woman, short and plump with an upsweep to her graying hair, tied in a bun on top. She is bringing a plate of veal cutlet with mashed potatoes from the stove and is placing it on the table in the kitchen. Seated at the table is a young man in a white intern's uniform. I'm the young man and the lady is my mother.

She sits down near me and is silent while I eat quickly since I have only a half-day off from the hospital near by. I tell my mother what has been on my mind for a long time. I tell her that I plan to become a plastic surgeon.

"What's that?"

"A surgeon who fixes scars, disfigurements, noses."

"Why does anyone have to have a nose fixed?"

I explain. She doesn't understand.

"Look, Max," she says. "What's this nonsense, plastic surgery?" (This is over thirty years ago.)

"It's a new kind of surgery."

"Are you crazy? Must you start something new? Where will you get patients? Who'll come to you?"

"They'll come."

"From the air? Dr. Schmargle brought you into the world. He's old now. You can be his assistant."

"I'm not interested in general practice."

"So be a plastic surgeon. But first marry a rich girl. You live in a two-family house. You have your office downstairs and you live upstairs. Then after fifteen years when you make a lot of money you can become a plastic surgeon."

"No, Ma. That's not the way to do it. You don't understand."

"Since when are you so smart? Are there many plastic surgeons?"

"A few. It's a new field."

"You'll starve!" She begins to weep. "If your father was alive." (Father was killed by an automobile when he was on his way to visit me at the hospital. He was anxious to see me in the white uniform of an intern. He never did.)

"Don't worry, Ma. You'll see. I'll be a plastic surgeon and I'll be successful."

I take her in my arms and I kiss her. She holds onto me for a while then lets me go.

This scene shows that as a young man I had a goal. Neither my family nor friends could talk me out of it. Their opinions didn't matter. My belief gave me confidence regardless of obstacles and I succeeded. My belief was so great that I was hypnotized by it.

FEAR

Now we see another scene. I've come back from Europe where I have studied plastic surgery for a year or more. I have opened up an office on lower Fifth Avenue near Eleventh Street and I wait for my first patient.

A week passes and there isn't a telephone call . . . except the one from my mother who asks me how I'm doing. The second week is the same as the first.

At the beginning of the third week I'm sitting near the window biting my nails. I'm watching a new apartment house going up across the street. A young husky man is carrying bricks on the fourth floor. I watch. He almost trips. And now I begin to imagine that sooner or later he will lose his balance and fall, and his face will be disfigured from this fall. I see myself rushing across the street and taking care of him on the spot. I see a big write-up in the newspapers and suddenly I am known. I watch this young man every day high up above the street but nothing happens. Not even a telephone call, except the one from Mother.

One more week and I have to pay the rent. The five-room suite now looks like a hundred rooms to me. Worry, fear suddenly overpower me. I see in my mind a picture of failure . . . I see myself closing the office . . . giving it up and pleading with Dr. Schmargle to let me work for him. I'm miserable. The vision of being a plastic surgeon becomes blurred in my mind. I'm in a panic.

At the beginning of the fourth week the phone rings. I dread to pick it up and speak to Mother. I pick it up. les a friend who became a doctor. He has a patient for me. I get shaved, put on my white coat. The hour is a lifetime before the doctor comes with my first patient. He is a shoe salesman in his twenties with a bashed-in nose from an accident.

I operate on him . . . and I know then that no matter what happens, no matter what the privations, the dream of becoming a plastic surgeon will come true.

THE ART OF DEHYPNOTIZING OURSELVES

So we see that at the beginning of my career I was hypnotized by a positive belief about my future even though many people didn't understand what this future was. The point is, I did. Yet, at a moment of fear and panic I was hypnotized by a negative belief that I'd never succeed. Hope made me stick it out and I succeeded. I dehypnotized myself from the negative belief that I would fail, as I dehypnotized myself from the negative belief when I was a second-year medical student and couldn't answer an oral question in pathology. I hypnotized myself by imagining I was looking through the microscope at a slide and wrote down what I saw, when asked a question orally the next time. I substituted a positive feeling for a negative one.

These negative feelings if persistent have exactly the same effect on behavior as the negative ideas implanted into the mind of a hypnotized person by a professional hypnotist.

Within all of us is the capacity for happiness, regardless of how big a failure we think we are, because within us is the power to change our feelings of inferiority by dehypnotizing ourselves from negative beliefs. We begin to dehypnotize ourselves from false beliefs the moment we stop trying to be what we're not, when we stop trying to be like someone else . . . by trying to be superior in an effort to overcome an inferiority complex. We are separate individual personalities, distinct from any other human being. We are not like the next person or in any way supposed to be like the other person. We are unique in ourselves We must stop keeping up with others. We must keep up with ourselves! We are not inferior or superior. We are we! Once we see this we are on the way of dehypnotizing ourselves from false feelings of inferiority.

We dehypnotize ourselves from the effects of stresses and strains by walking into the room of our mind and seating ourselves in our chair as we are now . . . seeing the geyser outside letting off steam . . . playing roles in our mind . . . watching motion pictures in our mind as we improve ourselves by being what we are and what we can be through the technique of relaxation: the greatest power within us to make us what we can be by teaching us to slough off the spasms and negative feelings that make us less than what we are. Relaxation is a form of hypnosis where we use our hidden powers to recall mental pictures of past scenes of happiness to make us happy for the present. Relax! Hypnotize yourself to happiness Dehypnotize yourself from extra worry, extra fear. Remember the words of John Dewey: "To me Faith means not worrying." Remember also what Johann Wolfgang Goethe said: "We are never deceived. We deceive ourselves."

Summary:

1. All our habits, good and bad, are daily forms of self-hypnosis.
2. Belief is a form of creative hypnotism.
3. Fear is also a form of hypnosis—negative hypnosis.
4. Our negative beliefs are the same as negative ideas implanted into the mind of a hypnotized person by a professional hypnotist.
5. We begin to dehypnotize ourselves from negative beliefs when we stop keeping up with the joneses; when we stop trying to be like someone else; when we become ourselves and keep up with ourselves!
6. We hypnotize ourselves usefully, creatively when we relax, and practice scenes in our mind, scenes of improving ourselves.
7. We thus hypnotize ourselves usefully, to a worthwhile purpose, to a goal of happiness.
8. It is well to remember the quotation of Mark Twain: "Don't part with your illusions. When they are gone, you may still exist but you may have ceased to live."

CHAPTER 11

THE SUCCESS MECHANISM . . . HOW IT WORKS

NOW WE IMAGINE we see another scene in the room of our mind.

The time . . . eight-thirty in the morning of any weekday. Thousands of people and hundreds of cars clog the streets. And now, swiftly and skillfully weaving through the congested traffic, a bicycle comes speeding along. The rider is not a messenger boy but a man . . . a slim good-looking man of thirty-five or so.

He pulls up to the curb halfway down the block, lifts the-bicycle, and carries it up one flight of stairs to his place of business. After storing the bicycle in the hallway, he removes the bicycle cuffs from his neat gray slacks, takes off his jacket, gives his hands a good scrubbing, and puts on his spotless white professional coat. Now he is ready for the day's business . . . trimming hair, shaving faces. For he is Frank Ferranti, the smiling barber of Forty-second Street.

At six-thirty in the evening Frank closes his shop, puts the bicycle cuffs on his trousers again, carries the bicycle downstairs, and starts for home. His route lies up Sixth Avenue to Central Park, through the Park to 110 Street and Fifth Avenue, over to Madison Avenue to the bridge across the Harlem River, then up Grand Concourse to 178 Street to the apartment house where he lives. He puts the bicycle in its regular spot in the basement and takes the elevator to the third floor where Rose Ferranti is waiting for him with her regular home-coming kiss . . . and dinner.

This scene demonstrates the first aspect of the success mechanisms sense of direction.

Functionally a man is like a bicycle. A bicycle maintains its poise and equilibrium only so long as it is going forward toward something. We cannot maintain our balance sitting still with no place to go.

We are built to achieve a goal, a sense of direction which means something to us. We must look forward, not backward. We must have a nostalgia for the future instead of for the past. The forward look will keep us young and happy. We must become interested in any kind of project because we want to.

Here are the aspects of the success mechanism that will work for us:

1. S: Sense of Direction
2. U: Understanding
3. C: Courage
4. C: Compassion
5. E: Esteem
6. S: Self-confidence
7. S: Self-acceptance

To illustrate these various ingredients of success let me tell you the following Story that took place in a far-off island in the Atlantic . . . the island of San Miguel in the Azores.

I am in an operating room in a hospital. Strong overhead lights cast no shadows. It is absolutely quiet. The anesthetist puts the patient under. He nods to me and I proceed to operate on the child, a little girl with a tumor over the left upper eyelid. A doctor and a nurse assist me. I remove the tumor to save the child's vision and to restore the child's face. Soon the operation is over.

And now the final scene a week after surgery before I leave the island. I am removing the bandages on the child's face for good. The child opens and closes her eyes. Both eyelids and eyebrows look the same. The child is happy as she looks into the mirror. The parents weep with happiness.

Now let us examine this operating-room scene as it applies to the success mechanism within us.

1. Sense of Direction.

When I proceeded to operate I had a sense of direction. I had a goal—to remove the tumor over the child's eyelid and eyebrow. And we, whoever we are, must have a daily goal in our lives, no matter how small or great, to make that day mean something. We remember the words of Ralph Waldo Emerson: "They can conquer who believe they can. It is he who has done the deed once who does not shrink from attempting it again."

2. Understanding.

I had understanding about the true nature of the problem. There was no confusion, and this should remind us that most of our failures in human relations are due to confusion . . . to misunderstanding. To avoid confusion and misunderstanding we must realize that it doesn't matter who is right but what is right. We must learn to admit our errors and mistakes without crying over them. During the operation I had to remove the tumor in a way different from what I had anticipated. I corrected my course and went forward. Remember the words of Anatole France: "It is better to understand a little than to misunderstand a lot."

3. Courage.

I had courage to remove the tumor regardless of consequences.

- We must have courage to bet on our ideas, to take the calculated risk, and to act. Everyday living requires courage if life is to be effective and bring happiness. We must have the courage to remove the tumor of doubt and resentment and the other negative aspects of the failure mechanism which we will discuss in the next chapter.

- We must study our own daily situations as if we were in an operating room ready to act and perform what we are capable of doing, by using our imagination to visualize the various courses of action possible and the consequences of each action. We then pick out the course offering the most promise and go ahead.

- We must take the risk of making a mistake in our relationship with others and then correct our course.

- We must not stand still. The success mechanism within all of us is ready to work for us but cannot guide us if we do nothing.

- We must not sell ourselves short.

- We must not try to be big heroes. It is more important to be little heroes every day by having the courage to face reality. Remember the words of Johann Schiller: "Who does nothing need hope for nothing."

4. Compassion.

I had to have compassion for the child to want to help. If we are to be happy and successful we must have this regard for others . . . remembering that we are part of the human family. We must respect the dignity of others, the fact that every person is a child of God. We must take the trouble to think of other people's feelings and viewpoints, their desires and needs. We must act as if other people are important and treat them accordingly . . . and when necessary, help them. Remember the words of Schopenhauer: "Compassion is the basis of all morality."

5. Esteem.

I had belief in myself when I operated on the child.

Several years ago I wrote a little essay about a quotation from Carlyle: "Alas the fearful unbelief is unbelief in yourself." Of all the traps and pitfalls in life, self-disesteem is the deadliest and the hardest to overcome; for it is a pit designed and dug by our own hands, summed up in the phrase, "It's no use-I can't do it."

The penalty of succumbing to it is heavy—both for the individual in terms of material rewards lost, and for society in gains and progress unachieved.

As a doctor I might also point out that defeatism has still another aspect, a curious one, which is seldom recognized. It is more than possible that the words quoted above are Carlyle's own confession of the secret that lay behind his own craggy assertiveness, his thunderous temper and waspish voice and his appalling domestic tyranny.

Carlyle, of course, was an extreme case. But isn't it on those days when we are most subject to the "fearful unbelief," that we most doubt ourselves and feel inadequate to our task—isn't it precisely then that we are most difficult to get along with?

We must stop carrying around a mental picture of ourselves as a defeated unhappy person. We must build an adequate self-image which means self-esteem . . . which does not mean egotism. Finally when we learn to respect others . . . that they are children of God and have some value, automatically our self-image improves, automatically our self-esteem rises, automatically we appreciate what we really are, and that is the beginning of happiness. It is well at this point to remember the words of the Greek philosopher Epictetus: "What I made I lost; what I gave I have."

When we give ourselves to others we never lose our self-respect.

6. Self-confidence.

I expressed self-confidence in operating on the child. Confidence is built on an experience of success. Each small success in our lives breeds success. I might say that for a moment I had trouble removing the tumor but I remembered the successful operations of the past and I worked toward my goal. At a moment of fear or uncertainty it is well for us to form the habit of remembering the past successes. The memory of this will sidetrack the memory of past failures and we thus permit our servomechanism to serve creatively with constructive results.

Practice improves in sports, also in the perfection of happy habits. Our electronic computer in our midbrain is prepared to remember the successes and forget the failures or errors. Our computer is prepared to remember the self-confidence of the past if we will only let it do its work. And this we can do by blocking off the memory of failures which bring with them fear, shame, remorse, guilt, which stifle self-confidence. No matter how many times we have failed in the past we must remember that all of us have succeeded in something sometime. We dwell on these feelings, happy feelings of self-confidence, when we are about to start a new undertaking. We rise above failures. Remember the words of John Dryden: "They can conquer who believe they can."

7. Self-acceptance.

I was happy indeed in bringing back the child to normal. I was happy because I did the best I could in my chosen field. I was myself.

Unhappiness and misery come when we try to be what we are not, masquerading with sham and pretense which exhaust our psychic reserve and mutilate our self image. If we are to be somebody we must learn to accept ourselves for what we are and do what we can do within the limits of our capabilities. And this does not mean limiting ourselves. Within our capabilities of self-confidence the future is limitless. This realization is the initial step in the development of an adequate image of ourselves. When we know this we can be more than we think we are when we neither underestimate nor overestimate ourselves . . . when we do not feel superior or inferior.

Self-acceptance comes when we are big enough to make peace with our mistakes without hiding behind deception. Once we know that we are not perfect we have a goal toward improvement. Only then do we become somebody. Only then do we become happy. Remember the words of George Bernard Shaw: "Better keep yourself clean and bright. You are the window through which you must see the world."

And finally, let me tell you this story. During my stay in the Azores, the Governor took me on a trip through the lush sunny green island, truly a fine jewel on this earth if ever there was one.

High in the mountains the Governor showed me the two magic lakes close to each other—one green, the other blue, telling me the legend of unrequited love of a shepherd and a king's daughter, concluding: "And these, the waters of the lakes, are supposed to be the tears of those two who died for love."

And then we passed through fertile hills. Blue hydrangeas were massed along the roadside, like gigantic leis. The warm white wings of windmills turned lazily in the warm breeze, cattle of an extraordinary plumpness grazed in the fields, and here was a whole acre of hothouses where the succulent pineapples of San Miguel were forced to extra plumpness and sweetness. Then came fields of tea and tobacco and areas which grew New Zealand ferns, Japanese camellias, and Scandinavian Abies. All this and more was explained to me by the Governor as well as by some of the men in the noisy retinue of motorcycles following its leader, dressed like the Charlie Chaplin of old with mustache and derby, on a jaunt to the town of Furnas.

Soon we looked down from the mountain and there buried in the green foliage was an awe-inspiring valley of steam. These were the famous Furnas geysers—the caldeiras —and the Governor said: "We of San Miguel are very lucky to have such rich soil and such good air to breathe. Much of the reason for it is in this valley. Don't you think, doctor, that a man too is something of an island?"

He expanded then on what he meant and later I left the valley of geysers thinking that his words were not so fanciful as they had seemed to me at first; no, I thought, they made good sense.

That night I was the guest at a party held in a wide garden open to the stars. I had a lot of wine and when called on to make a speech I jumped at the opportunity with alacrity.

I talked a bit then finally said: "Ladies and gentlemen, others may search far and wide for the secret of your beautiful island, why the air is so pure and the earth so young and bountiful and life so good, but I know what it is—there is no tension here. And why is that? Because in your wonderful Fumas valley, the geysers let it all out. And yes, men are like islands, as my good friend the Governor said. Let men relax from their daily tensions—let them even for a few minutes each day walk into a room in their mind and this room will be a garden with flowers—and with geysers outside—and let them relax—and see the geysers letting off steam, as your island does instead of bottling it up inside like anger, and these men will be happy; they will stay young, fresh and vigorous as your beautiful green island of San Miguel."

That is how the idea of the room in our mind to relax in was born. In conclusion let us make a habit to know ourselves; let us make a habit to know that there is a success mechanism within all of us that will make us happy if we daily recall the inspiring ingredients of the success mechanism that belong to us, that are rightfully ours.

1. S: Sense of Direction
2. U: Understanding
3. C: Courage
4. C: Compassion
5. E: Esteem
6. S: Self-confidence
7. S: Self-acceptance

CHAPTER 12

THE FAILURE MECHANISM

THE SUCCESS MECHANISM IS OUR GREEN LIGHT to move forward to our goal. The failure mechanism is our red light. It should make us stop, think, listen. It should be a signal to make a detour and to go toward our goal instead of stopping for good and forgetting our goal. With this resolution in mind it will be of great value to understand what the failure mechanism really is so that we can cope with it rather than be overcome by it . . . to turn a crisis into an opportunity. This will give us the will to make us stand up to our own statue of dignity and rise above failure, to achieve happiness. True happiness does not come only with success; it comes more with overcoming failure. Happiness comes not only from the good we do but from the harm we prevent to others and to ourselves. So let us study the ingredients of the failure mechanism.

The failure mechanism means tension spasm pressure. We learn to release this pressure by knowing the danger points, the signposts. We detour and take corrective action toward our destination. None of us are immune to negative feelings; the most successful people have them but they know them for what they are and they act to move in the right direction. Here are the main ingredients of the failure mechanism within us.

1. F: Fear: Frustration
2. A: Anger: Aggressiveness
3. I: Inferiority
4. L: Loneliness
5. U: Uncertainty
6. R: Resentment
7. E: Emptiness

1. Fear: Frustration.

Negative feelings happen like positive ones ... worry ... happiness. Worry is a form of fear frustration that appears when we try to solve a problem. We cure this and other failure symptoms not by will, but by understanding. When we do not achieve our goal, we become fearful, frustrated. But we must remember that we are never perfect and we will be dissatisfied now and then during our lifetime. We must learn to tolerate a certain amount of fear, frustration, without letting it overpower us.

- If we over respond to a frustrating experience with futility, it is a signal of failure.

- We must learn to see our self-image in proper perspective and we must correct this self-image ... if it is that of an unworthy, incompetent, inferior person who has no right to succeed.

- We have every right to be happy.

- We have every right to call upon our assets in our built-in success mechanism—when such crisis arises.

- We use our imagination and we feel as we did when we succeeded in the past ... and we feel that way now! Remember the words of Franklin Delano Roosevelt: "The only thing we have to fear is fear itself."

2. Anger: Aggressiveness.

Anger follows fear. Aggressiveness follows frustration. It is true that we need a certain kind of aggressiveness or determination to reach our goal.

- We must tackle problems aggressively, but constructively, if we are blocked in achieving our goal.
- We cannot use aggressiveness destructively—ignoring others, stepping on other people's toes.
- We do not remove aggressive traits but understand them in proper perspective in order to provide the proper channels for their expression.
- We cannot solve one problem by creating another.
- We get rid of our pent-up steam, our tension, by sitting in the room of our mind as we are doing right now. Or else we indulge in physical exercises: walking, tennis, golf. Or we write a letter giving vent to our anger, then tear it up. The best cure for aggressiveness is work—work toward a goal. Remember the words of Ralph Waldo Emerson: "A man should study ever to keep cool. He makes his inferiors his superiors by heat."

3. Inferiority.

This feeling of insecurity depends on our belief of our inadequacy.

- We must have no false measuring stick.
- We are goal strivers and we realize our true

potentialities when we move forward toward this goal every day, like a bicycle.

- We must never be satisfied and think we are perfect. This leads to insecurity.
- We must have a goal every day.
- We must stop fooling ourselves with the sham of being superior. This is self-defeating and inconsistent with our desire to go forward. Remember what Eleanor Roosevelt said: "No one can make you feel inferior without your consent."

4. Loneliness.

We all are lonely now and then, but to make a continual habit of it is failure. In this instance we walk away from ourselves and from our contact with others, from reality.

- We must be part of others. Doing things with others and enjoying it takes us away from ourselves . . . from the pretense that we can be alone.
- When we get to know others we lose our pretense and sham.
- Loneliness means limitation.
- Loneliness means unbelief in ourselves.
- Loneliness produces a nostalgia for an old yesterday. We must live in the present and for the present. When we are part of others, we become ourselves. Remember George Kelly's words: "People who live to themselves are generally left to themselves."

5. Uncertainty.

Uncertainty is a way of avoiding mistakes and we make the greatest mistake in life when we try to avoid making one.

- Decision-making need not be a life-and-death struggle.
- If we err we can correct our course tomorrow.
- We cannot be right all the time.
- Only little -men are never wrong.
- Continual uncertainty makes us unfit.
- Uncertainty makes us retreat. We must face life.
- We reach our true stature of dignity by rising above our failures, -not merely by achieving success. Remember the words of George Eliot: "No great deed is done By falterers who ask for certainty."

6. Resentment.

When we fail we are apt to blame society or someone.

- Resentment is an attempt to make our own failure palatable by shouting: "Unfair . . . unjust!"
- Resentment is the worst aspect of the failure mechanism because a great deal of energy is used negatively making happiness impossible.
- To the man who has resentment everyone is out of step but him.
- Of course some of us get false pleasure feeling wronged."
- Resentment can be a mental resistance to something

that has already happened and nothing is more debilitating than living continually in the past.

The trouble with resentment is that it becomes a bad habit that leads to self-pity, which is by far the worst negative habit of all, producing an inferior self-image . . . a scarred self-image . . . a distorted image. Resentment is caused by our own emotional response and leads to unhappiness and defeat. As long as we are resentful, we cannot see in us a self-reliant image, for we turn over the reins to others. It is inconsistent with creative goal-striving where we ourselves set the goal. Thus resentment means failure.

Now let me tell the following story as we sit in the room of our mind. I was on a lecture trip throughout California, and in Los Angeles I spoke before a thousand people at the First Church of Religious Science. My topic covered the success and failure mechanisms within us—how they work, not as separate entities but as interlocking opposing forces as we live our daily lives. I spoke about our assets, our liabilities, and how we can get more living out of life and be happy by being ourselves, by taking advantage of our assets.

During the question-and-answer period a stocky woman of forty got up and told the audience in a loud voice what my book Psycho-Cybernetics meant to her . . . how it made her become herself. I thanked her from the platform but she replied:

"Don't interrupt, doctor . . . I want to let you know what happened. I belong to a woman's charitable organization, and at special meetings the president of the society talks too much. Everyone fears her. And then I learned how to be myself and I want to thank you for your wonderful book. One evening at a meeting I decided to be myself. The president was talking on and on and I got up and said: 'Shut up."

The people in the audience laughed.

"You see, doctor, I was myself for the first time. I put her in her place."

"My dear lady," I said, "I fear you weren't yourself."

"What do you mean?" she asked. "I did what bad to be done."

"The trouble with your action is that you didn't read the book carefully. Your action had nothing to do with the book . . . you hated the woman . . . you used your resentment on her to get revenge. You were less than yourself! You begin to become yourself when you curb your hate your resentment—when you rise above it, when you rise above a negative destructive feeling."

It is well then to remember what Nietzsche said: "Nothing on earth consumes a man more quickly than the passion of resentment."

7. Emptiness.

When the capacity to enjoy is dead we find enjoyment in nothing. No goal is worth fighting for. And travel is no escape since it adds up to nothing. Happiness goes with creative goal-striving. It is possible to win a fake "success" but when we do we are penalized with an empty joy.

- Emptiness is a symptom of failure, a symptom that we are not living creatively, that we have no goal, that life has no purpose. People with goals find a meaning in life.

- Emptiness means the avoidance of effort and responsibility, and until we escape this vicious cycle by selecting some goal worth fighting for, we cannot achieve happiness.

- Emptiness means an inadequate self-image, and even if we overcompensate and achieve material success we feel a sense of guilt since our self-image is inadequate.

- Striving for goals which are important to us not as status symbols but which are consistent with our self-image is the beginning of happiness because it brings a deep inner satisfaction, Tolstoy said: "The only refuge from despair is to project one's ego into the world."

We must be aware of the liabilities within us that make us less than what we are . . . only to glance at them and understand why it is so important to focus on positive traits within us.

- We must be aware of the negatives only to stay clear of them.

- We should be sensitive to the negatives only to the extent that they alert us to danger.

- Each of the seven aspects of the failure mechanism abuses most the one who uses it.

- We recognize the negative for what it is, something we don't want since it does not bring happiness.

- We substitute a negative feeling for a positive one—the assets within us, our built-in success mechanism.

- We can make a habit of steering clear of the failure mechanism as much as we can make a habit of invoking the assets of the success mechanism to find happiness. Thomas Bailey Aldrich said: "They fail and they alone, who have not striven."

Summary:

1. F: Fear: Frustration. (We remember our courage.)
2. A: Anger: Aggressiveness. (We remember our compassion.)
3. I: Inferiority. (We are more than we think we are.)
4. L: Loneliness. (We need not be alone. We make the decision.)
5. U: Uncertainty. (We are not a mistake. We rise above it.)
6. R: Resentment. (Maturity begins when we rise above it.)
7. E: Emptiness. (We cannot be empty when we have a daily goal.)

CHAPTER 13

SUCCESS OR FAILURE?

NOW ASK YOU TO IMAGINE the following scenes as we sit in the room of our mind.

Scene 1—Thousands of birds high in the sky flying the cold North, migrating to warmer climate in the South.

Scene 2—A young squirrel born in June is gathering nuts in the fields. And now we see it hidden in a tree, hidden from the snow of January, eating nuts.

Scene 3—An infant, one year old, is trying to pick up a coin on a desk. His hand zigzags toward the coin and finally in a clumsy way he picks it up. Now we see the infant at the age of six picking up the coin on the desk accurately without the useless motion of muscles.

Scene 4—We see a boy of six selling newspapers on the East Side of Manhattan near the East River. It is a hot summer day and he is resting for a moment on a pier as he watches the sea gulls following the ships. Three older boys walk over to him, grab his papers, and throw him into the river. He never swam before, yet he paddles like a dog and manages to get back to the pier.

(I was that infant. I was that boy.)

The migrating birds and the squirrel prove that animals have a success mechanism within them, the will to survive, and pro-create the species. The birds fly to a warmer climate without a compass and the squirrel gathers nuts even before it ever knows that winter or snow exists. The infant picks up the coin in an awkward manner until he becomes successful in the performance of this act. This success is now registered in the electronic computing machine or tape recorder in the midbrain to be used thereafter in subsequent performances of picking up a coin. The unsuccessful way has been discarded.

Scene 5—I am with my mother a few years after starting my practice. I am located in a professional building on Fifty-seventh Street and Sixth Avenue. I am on the tenth floor and have five small rooms. I have been four years in practice; two on lower Fifth Avenue and two on the tenth floor of the medical building.

The owner of the building, who occupied the whole of the eighteenth floor, has passed away and at the suggestion of a trustee of the estate I am in the empty apartment and my mother is seated in a chair. She is catching her breath after walking through this huge apartment, ten times the size of my office on the tenth floor.

"It's such a big place, and such a big terrace," she says.

"You like?"

"What should I like about it? It would cost a fortune to fix up."

"I know," I answer. I hide my worry, my fear. To move is a tremendous risk. It may be too much. I may fail and the future may be black indeed.

"How much is the rent?" Mother asks.

"Ten times what I'm paying downstairs."

"Oh, my God," she sighs.

I'm crestfallen. I haven't the courage to forge ahead. I haven't the confidence. Doubt has overpowered me and I can think only of failure. I'm ready to agree with Mother as soon as she says I'm crazy.

"Well, Mom, what do you say?"

She thinks a minute then answers: "Well, Max, if you don't try at your age, when will you?"

I'm flabbergasted. "Mom, you were against the idea of plastic surgery."

"I didn't understand then and I still don't. But you do. You proved it. And I've all the confidence in the world in you.

We kiss. She cries. "If Dad only saw you now."

Scene 6—We now see my office and home on top of a medical building with terraces, rock gardens, and fourteen trees. And I've been there for thirty years.

a. The point is I had a goal within my capabilities, a sense of direction, and nothing could keep me from this goal, and this is one of the most important means of letting the success mechanism within us work for us, uninhibited . . . provided we have the training and experience for this goal.

b. I had anxiety before making the change. My mother gave me the necessary encouragement. Once I made the decision I stuck to it and stopped worrying.

c. My mother, who worried for me when I started practice, realized that I succeeded in my chosen field. She realized she had made a mistake about me. Profiting by this error she encouraged me to take the calculated risk for my future.

d. Thus animals and humans have the success mechanism within them but there is one tremendous difference with humans. We have the forebrain, which gives us the desires beyond survival and procreation of the species, which gives us the emotional and spiritual insight to create ideals to live by. This is a demonstration of my teachings of what I call Psycho-Cyberneties.

Now let us visualize —the summary of this chapter, which indicates how the success mechanism works for us if we let it.

1. We must relax while doing our job. This is the reason why we are in the room of our mind for five minutes every day.. . to make a happy habit of it.
2. We must think of the pros and cons before our

undertaking. Here we make use of worry, fear, or anxiety to select what is best for us and once we make the decision we stick to it, refusing to permit worry to jam our creative success mechanism, which was given to us by our Creator to make us succeed in reaching our goal.

3. We must learn to do one thing at a time.

4. If we are stymied and cannot reach a conclusion we must let matters rest for a while. We must sleep on it . . . and the next morning or later our success mechanism will help us find the answer to our problem or else we will see to it that we are not sidetracked from our goal by negative feelings. We must keep our eye on the ball.

5. We must make a habit of reacting to the present moment spontaneously. Every day must be a composite lifetime in itself. Our creative mechanism will work for us now if we let it . . . not tomorrow. We must respond to the immediate twenty-four hours of today by keeping our eyes and ears open to our environment, remembering our goal for that day. We must not respond to the past where we failed . . . to the same environment of the past unless this negative feedback makes us modify our course, not stop it; unless the past was a happy experience that gave us confidence.

6. We must stop criticizing ourselves.

7. Relaxation in the room of our mind is our daily vacation, our built-in tranquilizer that teaches us not to over respond to negative feelings, but rather not respond at all like not answering the telephone when it rings.

8. We turn a crisis into an opportunity by acting aggressively as we keep our goal in mind.

9. We keep a crisis in proper perspective. We don't make a mountain out of a molehill.

10. Under these circumstances we let a bell ring—a reminder to change the negative into the positive.

These ten tools make up our first-aid kit which helps us reach our goal. They are the keys to happiness. They open the door to a better and fuller life.

Without them we jam the lock on the door with our spastic fingers, locking ourselves within ourselves, preventing us from opening the door to opportunity. We stay in a dark room inhibited, permitting the failure mechanism within us, the stranger within, the evil twin within us to work like a gangster to make us less than we are and this means *Unhappiness*.

There is an old Irish proverb: "If God shuts one door, He opens another." If we are filled with frustration we cannot weep about it . . . we cannot plead to God to take us out of our misery; to lift us up and take us into another room of opportunity. God helps those who help themselves. We must stand with our hand on the knob of the door ready to open the door to a new room of opportunity ourselves!

Remember these two other quotations:

Elbert Hubbard said: "A failure is a man who has blundered, but is not able to cash in on the experience."

Edgar Guest wrote: "He started to sing as he tackled the thing That couldn't be done and he did it."

CHAPTER 14

HOW TO SPREAD HAPPINESS

L ET ME TELL YOU THREE DIFFERENT STORMS which, though not connected, have an inspirational point in common. Story 1: Digging near a vegetable growing village on the east coast of Attica, Dr. John Papadimitriou, Director of Antiquities in Greece's Ministry of Education, recently uncovered fifteen wooden vases carved in geometrical designs—the first such find in history. Knowing that fresh air would decompose the wood which had been preserved in fertile mud since the fifth and sixth centuries B.C., the archeologist rushed them twenty-three miles to Athens for a thorough preservation bath.

Also Professor John L. Casky of the University of Cincinnati has found in Greece a Mycenean settlement dating back 3500 years complete with temple, palace, private homes with inside plumbing, and a municipal sewer system.

And so from time to time we learn of new excavations that bring old civilizations to light.

How useful it would be if we dug a little inside ourselves. We don't need an ax or a shovel or any instrument for that matter. All we need is five minutes a day when we rest after a day's work in the room of our mind. We use these five minutes to concentrate on ourselves. Concentration is thought in action. A thought has a middle, a beginning, and an ending. We reflect on our fears, our unbeliefs, on our failures . . . and we reflect logically . . . one thing at a time with a beginning, a middle, and an ending and then we come to the sudden realization that we are not our mistakes or failures, that we have assets too, and that we must not allow our assets—our dignity and self-respect to be buried under our mistakes. If we understand ourselves a little better we can rem(we the debris of failure and we are sure to find treasures more important to us than the treasures found by bygone civilizations. We begin to find out more about ourselves.

These treasures are our dignity, our sincerity, our understanding; our self-confidence and courage that we must uproot within ourselves to help us tackle life's problems, to help us reach our daily goal to give us the proper image which in turn brings happiness.

Story 2: Recently a woman consulted me about removing some of the signs of aging from her face. She wondered if she was doing the right thing coming to my office in secret without letting the family know.

"Why didn't you tell them?" I asked.

"They'd be against it. My husband and married daughter would consider me vain and foolish."

I explained that in thirty years of practice as a plastic surgeon I had never seen a case of vanity . . . that patients with disfigurements, child and adult alike, seek the aid of the plastic surgeon for psychological and social reasons, if not for economic reasons. Actually they want a disfigurement removed because they want a second chance in life.

She said: "That's it, doctor. I want a second chance. I want to look as best I can to my husband and daughter . . . and grandchildren."

"Well, explain it to your family," I suggested.

I subsequently operated on this lady and while she was in the hospital she confessed she didn't know how to speak to her husband and had the operation done on her own. She got an excellent result but her husband was furious and unforgiving.

Unfortunately we spend too much time with negative traits like unforgiveness which scars our inner self-image, distorting us more than the few wrinkles on the face. And these disfiguring wrinkles within are easy to remove without the aid of plastic surgery by the mere act of forgiveness. We all deserve a second chance in life regardless of our years or of our mistakes. And we give ourselves another chance through forgiveness forgiveness with no strings attached, a clean slate. Thus we remove our emotional scars and give another chance not only to someone else but to ourselves.

The most difficult aspect of forgiveness is not so much forgiving someone else as forgiving ourselves. A sense of guilt is one of the great tragedies in living . . . but one of the joys of living is to rise above guilt, above the mistakes and frustrations of yesterday. This brings happiness.

We also must remember that we are not responsible for the mistakes of others. We must remember that creative living every day means the right we have to give ourselves another chance to improve ourselves and circumvent the same mistakes in the future. If we do that, and we should, we give ourselves an emotional face lift. We remove our inner scar, the wrinkles on the face of our inner image, without the need of plastic surgery.

Story 3: During the year 1630, a deadly plague swept through the old city of Milan, in Italy. Hundreds of different—and outlandish—treatments and remedies were used by the city's physicians, but nothing served to stem the dreadful tide of contagion. And with the physical sickness came a disease that was even more loathsome, and even more proof against any remedy. That was the disease of suspicion.

Surely, said those of the city's citizens who remained alive, surely this plague cannot be explained by natural causes, or else it would have died out long ago, as other plagues raged and then swiftly died. This plague is like no other. It is so deadly, and so persistent, that someone among us must be responsible for it—some monstrous evildoer who is secretly nourishing the plague and spreading it farther and farther.

One morning the Commissioner of Health of Milan, the eminent Gughehno Piazza, went out into the city to write down notes and observations on the present state of the plague. He took with him a horn container full of ink, and as he walked along the festering streets he wrote down all that he saw. A number of times he stained his fingers with ink and, to clean them, rubbed them against the wall of a house.

An old woman crouched in one of the houses saw him cleaning his fingers in this manner, and farther on, someone else saw him clean his fingers again. But they did not think that he was doing anything so simple. They saw the black smears left on the walls, and the disease of suspicion in their minds flamed forth in a great uprush of fear and hate; and they cried out, Look! See what this devil in human form is doing! He is spreading the plague!"

There is no defense against ignorance well, at least there was none then. Whatever Gugliehno Piazza said was disbelieved; his simple, true explanation was shouted down; he was cursed and filth was thrown at him; and then he was forced to undergo such horrible tortures that he could no longer sustain himself against them; and so, to escape the torture, he lied. He said that yes, he had been spreading the plague.

For this, Guglieh—no Piazza was burned at the stake. And, of course, the pestilence still raged.

This sad tale of ignorance and suffering and barbarous death took place only a trifle more than three hundred years ago. Some two hundred and fifty years afterward, medical science discovered that human beings could in fact spread a plague—but all unwittingly, not knowing that they were serving as agents of destruction. One such person, whose name was Mary, left behind her a wake of disease and death—typhoid. Mary carried the germ of typhoid without being affected by it herself. And so the name came into being, "Typhoid Mary," standing for one who spreads a communicable disease.

We have all heard of these communicable diseases communicable death. But have you heard of communicable happiness?

Yes, communicable happiness exists too. And there are Typhoid Marys of Happiness—people who spread communicable health. Undoubtedly you have met one, perhaps without knowing it. But there are certain signs whereby they can be recognized. These signs are:

1. A sense of direction
2. Sincerity and understanding
3. Compassion
4. Courage
5. Self-respect
6. Confidence
7. Self-acceptance
8. Cheerfulness
9. Optimism. Belief in the future
10. Faith in God, faith in themselves
11. A desire and a will and a never-failing, positive ability to help others

These are the Typhoid Marys of Happiness. They spread health and, by spreading it, are even more infected by health and happiness themselves.

We all can have these qualifications. We can make them our own, one by one, and become a Typhoid Mary of Happiness. We remember the three stories just told. We too become a Typhoid Mary of Happiness when we dig beneath our mistakes and find treasures underneath—our assets, that give us the means to achieve happiness and spread this happiness to others. We too become the Typhoid Mary of Happiness when we forgive others and ourselves for errors, without strings attached, when we give others and ourselves a second chance . . . a second chance that we are entitled to. We thus bring happiness to ourselves and we spread it to others.

How important it is today to discover the secrets of outer space. How more important it is, perhaps, to discover the inner space of our mind . . . to ferret out the guilt and hurt feelings that distort our self-image and make us less than what we are . . . to rise above failure, to discover that we are more successful not from the successes we achieve but from the failures we surmount. It brings happiness . . . a happiness we are anxious to share with others, to spread to others.

This should teach us one of the great lessons in living . .

. namely, that we can be enriched and ennobled by our scars rather than destroyed by them. We then become a Typhoid Mary of Happiness. We then become part of a great adventure—the Adventure in Staying Young! Remember the words of Horace: "Seize now and here the hour that is, nor trust some later day."

And if we become a Typhoid Mary of Happiness and then infect only ten others—and they in turn infect ten more—think how rapidly communicable health and happiness can spread all over the world!

In conclusion I believe it is important to repeat the words of judge Jonah Goldstein:

"Happiness is the only product in the world that multiplies by division."

FREE AUDIO DOWNLOAD FROM THE PSYCHO-CYBERNETICS FOUNDATION

As a purchaser of this book, you are entitled to a free audio copy of *The Happiness Secret No One Seems to Know,* which introduces you to advanced principles in *Psycho-Cybernetics* that I teach to my private clients. Simply email me directly at matt@mattfurey.com and request a link to the free audio download.

You can also greatly benefit from the riveting, information-packed emails we regularly send out regarding self-image psychology and improved brain performance. To be on our email list, visitpsycho-cybernetics.com today.

Additionally, if you're curious about accelerating your development by being coached in the life-changing principles of *Psycho-Cybernetics*, visit psycho-cybernetics.com and fill out our coaching application.

9 781722 500313